BLACK BOOK OF

NEW YORK

*The Essential Guide to the
Quintessential City*

BEN GIBBERD

MAPS BY DAVID LINDROTH INC.

ILLUSTRATED BY
KERREN BARBAS STECKLER

PETER PAUPER PRESS, INC.
WHITE PLAINS, NEW YORK

FOR NINA AND JACK,
TRUE NEW YORKERS

*The editors would like to extend a special
thanks to cartographer David Lindroth
for his tireless efforts on this project.*

Updated by Arielle Datz and Margaret Littman

Designed by Heather Zschock

Illustrations copyright © 2016 Kerren Barbas Steckler

The Map is copyrighted by the MTA. Used by permission.
Neighborhood maps © 2016 David Lindroth Inc.

Copyright © 2016
Peter Pauper Press, Inc.
202 Mamaroneck Avenue
White Plains, NY 10601
All rights reserved
ISBN 978-1-4413-1888-6
Printed in Hong Kong
7 6 5 4 3 2 1

Visit us at www.peterpauper.com

THE LITTLE
BLACK BOOK OF
NEW YORK

CONTENTS

INTRODUCTION

New York City is immense, the biggest city in the United States and one of the biggest in the world, with a population of more than eight million covering 305 square miles. It's packed with some of the most famous restaurants, museums, buildings, and visitor sites in the world. Our pocket-sized *Little Black Book of New York* covers the top picks for each neighborhood, in an easy-to-use and unintimidating format for those new to the city. You can take this book with you anywhere in Manhattan—knowing it will provide a succinct list of what's essential in every neighborhood, from art galleries to architecture—and because of its size, most people won't even know you're a tourist!

We've broken Manhattan down by neighborhoods, and then grouped adjoining neighborhoods into eight individual maps and chapters for convenience; there's also a public transportation map at the back. If you'd rather look things up by their specific names, we've included an index, too. We hope you enjoy your visit, and that you'll find all you need in this *Little Black Book* to navigate this great city with pleasure and aplomb.

NEW YORK STREET GRID

New York is a pretty easy city to get around, thanks to its grid plan that was adopted in 1811. The plan called for 12 numbered avenues running north and south roughly parallel to the Hudson River, and about

155 cross streets running east and west. Exceptions to this plan include Broadway, which was in place at the time of the 1811 plan. It cuts an angle from southeast to northwest. Rather than change it, this was turned to the city's advantage by creating "squares" wherever Broadway crossed a north-south avenue. The famed Broadway is now practically synonymous with New York City. Greenwich Village (below 14th Street) was also able to keep its confusing street pattern (largely because it had been kept separate from the rest of the city by a yellow fever and cholera epidemic in the early 1800s). The streets of the Village are for the most part the same as they were in the early 1800s, with crooked paths best suited for walking. The winding roads can make this area a bit challenging to navigate, but the charming cobblestone streets are well worth it.

HOW TO USE THIS GUIDE

We have included eight fold-out maps, by neighborhood sections, with color-coded keys to help you find the places listed in the text. **Red** symbols indicate **Places to See**, which include landmarks, arts and entertainment, and fun stuff to do with kids. **Blue** symbols indicate **Places to Eat & Drink**, which include restaurants, bars, and nightlife. Orange symbols indicate Where to Shop. And **Green** symbols indicate **Where to Stay**.

Here are our keys for restaurant and hotel costs:

Restaurants

Cost of an appetizer and main course without drinks

($)	Up to $25
($$)	$25-$45
($$$)	$45-$70
($$$$)	$70 and up

Hotels

Cost per night

($)	$50-$125
($$)	$125-$250
($$$)	$250-$400
($$$$)	$400 and up

PUBLIC TRANSPORTATION

The public transportation map at the back lets you know how to get around fast and easily on the subways. We've started each neighborhood section with a listing of which subways (and subway stops) to use to get to the neighborhood.

A free copy of the subway map is available at any subway station booth. The main way to pay for public transportation is the MetroCard, a magnetic fare card, which is sold at all subway station booths, and through vending machines (that accept cash, debit, and credit cards) that are in many subway stations and at many other locations. You can use a MetroCard at all subway stations and on all public and many private buses within New York City. If you use a MetroCard, you can transfer free of charge between subway and bus, bus and subway, bus and bus. Seven- to 30-day unlimited ride MetroCards are also available.

In addition to the subway, New York now has a Citi Bike system (more info at www.citibikenyc.com). You can get a 24-hour or 7-day pass at any Citi Bike station, located throughout the city, and then ride around for 30-minute stretches at a time.

SUBWAY TIPS

Listen Up

As with any mass public transportation system, there are bound to be service changes, repairs, interruptions, etc. Don't panic! Just listen to the conductors for their specific directions, read the signs posted, and don't be afraid to ask other passengers questions. New Yorkers (contrary to their bad rap) are helpful and love to dispense directions to show off their New York knowledge.

Downtown-Uptown

When you're entering a subway station, pay attention to whether you're using the "Downtown" entrance or the "Uptown" entrance. They're usually right across the street from each other. You don't want to end up paying twice because you went through the wrong entrance! Some of the bigger stations don't split their entrances on the street level (for example, Times Square). In those cases, you can choose the uptown or downtown side once you get underground.

SEASONAL EVENTS

In spring, flowers bloom and New Yorkers come out to play. Summer can be hot and humid, and with many residents retreating to the country or the shore, it's easier to get a table at that exclusive restaurant or to grab an otherwise tough ticket on Broadway. Fall offers some of the most beautiful weather of the year, and the occasional chill foretells the arrival of winter, when sparkling snow and city lights combine to create a true wonderland. No matter the season, the Big Apple offers world-class entertainment, sports, and special events.

Spring:

St. Patrick's Day Parade (March 17th)—Just days before the official start of spring, "New York's Finest" come out in droves for the annual parade. Fifth Avenue becomes a sea of police officers, firefighters, and plenty of leprechauns to celebrate the green holiday *(Fifth Ave, 44th to 86th Sts., www.nycgo.com/events/st.-patricks-day-parade, starts at 11AM).*

Easter Parade (Easter Sunday)—No longer limited to the elite showing off their holiday finery, the parade that inspired the song marches up Fifth Avenue between 49th and 57th, starting at 10AM *(www.nycgo.com)*. Put on your own Easter bonnet—with all the frills upon it—and join in. Or just sit back and watch the spectacle.

Play Ball! (Early April)—Unless you have several free hours, never ask a Yankee fan why their team is better than the Mets (or vice versa). Whichever team you choose to root for, Opening Days for the fabled **New York Yankees** *(newyork.yankees.mlb.com, 718-293-4300)* or **New York Mets** *(newyork.mets.mlb.com, 718-507-TIXX)* are a sure sign of spring. For a more intimate experience, cheer on one of New York's minor league teams. The **Brooklyn Cyclones**, Class A affiliate of the Mets, play at KeySpan Park on New York's famous Coney Island *(www.brooklyncyclones.com, 718-372-5596)*. Or catch a great game along with unparalleled views of the Manhattan skyline watching the Staten Island Yankees *(www.siyanks.com, 718-720-9265)*. The Yankees Class A farm team plays at Richmond County Bank Ballpark at St. George, which is located just steps away from the **Staten Island Ferry**, the best ferry bargain in town.

Summer:

Street Fairs (Every weekend from late spring to early fall on various streets)—Throughout summer, New Yorkers reclaim numerous city streets from taxis, buses, and bike messengers, by converting them into lively street fairs— perfect for pedestrians to have free rein. They offer a mix of merchandise, classic street fair food, live entertainment, and great people watching *(www.nycstreetfairs.com)*.

Shakespeare in the Park (June–August)—New York likes to air out Shakespeare every summer. See stars like Meryl Streep and Al Pacino and many more perform Shakespeare's plays at the Delacorte Theater in Central Park. Tickets are free (limit 2 per person), but they go fast *(212-539-8500, www.publictheater.org for schedule)*.

New York Philharmonic (July)—The nation's oldest symphony orchestra performs outdoor concerts in all five boroughs during the summer *(www.nyphil.org)*.

Summer Friday Music Concerts (June–August)—Catch the stars out in the daytime! The network morning shows are in a battle for ratings and for the best concert acts, which you can catch for free outside on summer Fridays. ABC's *Good Morning America* broadcasts their concerts from Central Park *(www.abcnews. go.com/GMA)*, and NBC's *Today Show* broadcasts in Rockefeller Plaza *(49th Street between 5th and 6th Aves., www.todayshow.com)*.

Autumn:

Broadway on Broadway (mid-September)—The Broadway season starts in September. The League of American Theaters kicks it off every year with a free outdoor concert in Times Square showcasing highlights of the new offerings *(details in August at www.broadwayonbroadway. com)*. Like what you see? Reduced price theater tickets are available the day of the performance at the Theater Development Fund's "TKTS" booths, located in Times Square and at the South Street Seaport *(www.tdf.org, credit cards, cash, and travelers checks accepted)*.

Village Halloween Parade (October 31st, evening)—In New York's Greenwich Village, they take Halloween to the extreme. The annual Halloween parade displays New York at its craziest *(on 6th Ave. between Spring and 21st Sts., www.halloween-nyc.com, starts at 7PM)*.

Macy's Thanksgiving Day Parade (November)—Giant balloons, marching bands from around the country, and the arrival of Santa! A New York tradition since 1924, the parade steps off at 77th St. and Central Park West, then continues down Broadway all the way to Macy's flagship store in Herald Square at 34th Street *(www. macys.com/parade)*. If you're not up for the parade, watch them inflate the giant balloons the night before, along Central Park West *(77th/81st Sts., usually from 3PM to 10PM)*.

New York City Marathon (early November)—Each year, about 85,000 runners from around the world wind their way through all five boroughs, to the big finish in Central Park. And all along the way, two million people line the streets to cheer them on *(www.tcsnyc marathon.org)*.

Winter:

Christmas Tree at Rockefeller Center (lighted the week after Thanksgiving at 7PM)—The annual lighting of the Rockefeller Center Christmas Tree marks the official start of the holiday season. Carefully chosen following a nation-wide search (they even transported one from Ottawa, Canada, in 1966), the tree—traditionally a Norway Spruce (65 to 90 feet tall)—is brought to Rockefeller Plaza in November, trimmed, and lighted in a gala ceremony the week after Thanksgiving. While at Rockefeller Center, strap on some skates and show your stuff at the **Rockefeller Center Ice Rink** *(Fifth to Sixth Aves., 49th/50th Sts., 212-332-7654, www.rockefellercenter.com)*.

George Balanchine's The Nutcracker™ (November–January)—E. T. A. Hoffmann's classic tale comes to life with George Balanchine's magical production of *The Nutcracker* performed by the **New York City Ballet** *(Lincoln Center, 212-496-0600, www.nycballet.com).*

Radio City Christmas Spectacular (November–January)—Rockettes fill the stage for this annual high-kicking Christmas performance, which has been celebrated for over 75 years *(Radio City Music Hall, 6th Ave., 50/51st Sts., 866-858-0007, www.radiocity.com).*

New Year's Eve Ball Drop (December 31st)—Ring in the new year in Times Square with its famous ball-dropping countdown. You'll be showered with confetti and cheers. Just be prepared to get intimate with your neighbors—quarters are tight, and security's even tighter *(Times Square, 43rd/Broadway, check website for street entrances: www.timessquarenyc.org).*

NEW YORK'S TOP PICKS

TOP PICK!

New York offers an abundance of one-of-a-kind attractions and experiences for visitors. Here are 13 of the top picks not to be missed!

* ★ Ellis Island *(see page 21)*
* ★ Statue of Liberty *(see page 21)*
* ★ South Street Seaport *(see page 25)*
* ★ Brooklyn Bridge *(see page 37)*
* ★ **Chinatown** *(see page 41)*
* ★ **Times Square** *(see page 114)*
* ★ Empire State Building *(see page 136)*
* ★ Rockefeller Center *(see page 137)*
* ★ St. Patrick's Cathedral *(see page 138)*
* ★ Grand Central Terminal *(see page 139)*
* ★ Museum of Modern Art (MoMA) *(see page 140)*
* ★ Metropolitan Museum of Art *(see page 176)*
* ★ **Central Park** *(see page 185)*

chapter 1

FINANCIAL DISTRICT
BATTERY PARK CITY
TRIBECA
CIVIC CENTER

Places to See:

1. Wall Street
2. Trinity Church
3. New York Stock Exchange
4. St. Paul's Chapel
5. Ground Zero
6. Bowling Green
7. Battery Park/Ferries
8. Wall Street Bull
9. National Museum of the American Indian
10. New York City Police Museum
11. ELLIS ISLAND ★
12. STATUE OF LIBERTY ★
13. Staten Island Ferry/ Whitehall Ferry Terminal
14. South Street Seaport Museum
15. Fraunces Tavern Museum
26. Waterfront
27. North Cove Yacht Harbor
28. Winter Garden/World Financial Center
29. Museum of Jewish Heritage
30. Esplanade
31. Nelson A. Rockefeller Park
32. Robert F. Wagner, Jr. Park
36. Duane Park
37. New York Mercantile Exchange Building
38. apexart
39. Soho Photo Gallery
40. Tribeca Performing Arts Center
56. City Hall
57. Municipal Building
58. Woolworth Building
59. BROOKLYN BRIDGE ★

Places to Eat & Drink:

16. BLT Bar & Grill
17. Harry's Cafe & Steak
18. Delmonico's
19. Trading Post
20. Alfanoose Middle Eastern Cuisine
21. Haru
22. The Full Shilling
33. Terry's Deli
34. Liberty View Restaurant
41. Edward's

★ Top Picks

Chicago, Boston, Detroit,
they're all the same,
except New York...
that is a city!

—*Eve Minard, in* For Me and My Gal *(1942)*

FINANCIAL DISTRICT

④⑤ *to Wall St.;* **②③** *to Wall St.*

● SNAPSHOT ●

Manhattan Island was settled by Europeans, moving south to north, so the oldest neighborhoods are here in what is called Lower Manhattan. At the southern tip is Battery Park, one of New York's oldest public open spaces. More than four million people annually visit the park and its major landmark, Castle Clinton National Monument. Wall Street—so named for the defensive wall that stood here when this area was a Dutch town in the 1600s—and the adjacent financial center are now the financial hub of New York. Although this area has become increasingly residential, with more bars, restaurants, and other amenities than ever before, it's still mostly thought of as a place to work.

PLACES TO SEE
Landmarks:

Wall Street (1) runs east of Broadway to South Street, and was originally a wooden wall built by the Dutch marking the city's northernmost edge. Although the city's financial institutions are now spread over a much wider area (especially post 9/11), this district is still the epicenter of the country's finances. Walking west, check out **Trinity Church (2)** *(Broadway/Wall Sts., 212-602-0800 www.trinitywallstreet.org, admission free)*, a beautiful Gothic Revival structure that offers lunchtime concerts *(see www.trinitywallstreet.org for concert details*

19

and opening times), with its adjacent churchyard where such notables as Alexander Hamilton are buried. The arch temple to Mammon with its columned portico, the **New York Stock Exchange (3)** *(11 Wall Street, Broad/ New Sts.)* unfortunately has been closed to the public since 9/11. Other nearby landmarks are the lovely 18th-century **St. Paul's Chapel (4)** *(209 Broadway, Fulton/Vesey Sts., 212-602-0800, www.saintpaulschapel.org; hours: M– Sa 10AM–6PM, Su 7AM–6PM)*, which houses George Washington's original pew, and, of course, **Ground Zero (5)** *(Liberty/Vesey Sts., west of Church St.)*, former site of the World Trade Center towers. Open since May 2014, the **9/11 Memorial Museum** *(1 Albany St. at Greenwich St., 212-266-5211, www.911memorial.org; hours: open daily at 9AM–8PM)* pays tribute to the almost 3,000 people killed in the attacks on the World Trade Center. Advance reservations are required. **One World Observatory** *(285 Fulton St., www.oneworldobservatory.com)* recently opened at the top of the tallest building in the Western Hemisphere. It is located on the 100th, 101st, and 102nd level of One World Trade Center. One World Observatory will offer views of New York City's iconic sights, surrounding waters, and skyline. The experience will go beyond the view as guests can explore three levels of the Observatory filled with innovation, videos, and inspiration. Farther south are two oases of green amid the canyons, tiny **Bowling Green (6)** at the foot of Broadway and **Battery Park (7)** *(south of Battery Place)*, where the **Ferries (7)** to Ellis Island and the Statue of Liberty depart *(see pages 21–22)*.

Arts & Entertainment:

At **Bowling Green (6)**, you'll find the famous bronze statue of the **Wall Street Bull (8)**. Also at Bowling Green is the **National Museum of the American Indian (9)** *(1 Bowling Green, State/Whitehall Sts., 212-514-3700, www.nmai.si.edu, free admission; hours: daily 10AM–5PM, Th until 8PM)*, housed in the Beaux Arts former U.S. Custom House Building. The collection features thousands of works from textiles to carved stone heads. And the building itself, with its painted ceilings and great atrium, is worth the visit alone. The **New York City Police Museum (10)** *(45 Wall St., Broad/William Sts., 646-287-3080, www.nycpolicemuseum.org; temporarily closed for renovations, check website for updates)* with its re-created crime scenes, complete with chalk body outlines and fake drug stashes, is more than a little hokey, but it's also one of the city's most charming and fascinating small museums. ★**ELLIS ISLAND (11)** *(see below)*, with its wonderful immigration museum, and the ★**STATUE OF LIBERTY (12)** *(see page 22)* on Liberty Island, can both be reached by ferry from Castle Clinton National Monument, a circular sandstone fort in Battery Park *(for advance tickets call 866-782-8834)*. The ancestors of almost half of today's Americans entered the country through ★**ELLIS ISLAND (11)** *(212-363-3200, www.nps.gov/elis; hours: daily 9AM–5PM, closed Dec. 25th)*. More than 12 million new Americans passed through this immigration portal from 1892 to 1954. Visitors get a taste of the real experience by walking through the Baggage Room (where the immigrants would first arrive

TOP PICK!

and drop off their belongings), or sitting in the Registry Room. There are also interactive audio exhibits where you can hear immigrants speak of their experiences passing through Ellis Island. In addition, visitors can learn about the island's rich past and research their own family's immigration history.

You are also welcome to get up close to the ★STATUE OF LIBERTY (12) *(212-363-3200, www.nps.gov/stli; hours: daily 9:30AM–5PM, closed Dec. 25th)*, which greeted most of those newcomers arriving through Ellis Island. Standing as tall as a 22-story building, she has guarded New York Harbor since 1886. A gift of friendship from France, she is an international symbol of freedom. Photographs, oral histories, prints, and videos are displayed on the 2nd floor. They cover the history and symbolism of the statue throughout the years. You can also take the free Staten Island Ferry (13)—the city's best bargain—to Staten Island and back from the contemporary glass Whitehall Ferry Terminal (13) *(end of Whitehall St. at the water, 718-815-BOAT, www.siferry. com)*. The South Street Seaport Museum (14) *(Visitors' Center: 12 Fulton St. at South St., 212-748-8600, www. southstreetseaportmuseum.org; daily 11AM–6PM)* maintains a great collection of old sailing ships lining the dock. You can also view re-creations of printing shops and 19th-century craftsmanship. The Fraunces Tavern Museum (15) *(54 Pearl St. at corner of Broad St., 212-425-1778, www.frauncestavernmuseum.org; hours: M–Su 12PM–5PM)* opened to the public in 1907. The original tavern was a meeting ground for the Sons of Liberty in the pre-revolutionary years, and became the site in which Washington gave his farewell speech at the end of the war.

Kids:

The **South Street Seaport Museum (14)** has programs for kids and families. Check out "Family Programs" on its website, *www.southstreetseaportmuseum.org*, for details. Amid the cobblestone streets of the seaport, there are also plenty of street performers drawing crowds and needing young volunteers for spectacular stunts and magic tricks. Take your kids on a ferry to see "Lady Liberty" up close. Buy tickets at Castle Clinton in **Battery Park (7)** *(see page 20)*. And if you have young aspiring crime fighters in your family, they'll enjoy the **New York City Police Museum (10)** *(see page 21)*.

PLACES TO EAT & DRINK
Where to Eat:

Housed in a W Hotel, **BLT Bar & Grill (16) ($$$)** *(123 Washington St. at Albany St., 646-826-8666; www. e2hospitality.com/blt-bar-grill-new-york; hours: daily 7AM–10PM)* the playful (yet elegant) restaurant—puts unexpected twists on traditional fare. **Harry's Cafe & Steak (17) ($$)** *(1 Hanover Sq. at Pearl St., 212-785-9200, www.harrysnyc.com; kitchen hours: M–F 11:30AM–12AM, Sa 11AM–12AM, bar until 2AM)* is a classic steakhouse noted for its aged strip steak, wine cellar, and brunch. **Delmonico's (18) ($$$$)** *(56 Beaver St. at South William St., 212-509-1144, www.delmonicosny.com; hours: M–F 11:30AM–10PM, Sa 5PM–10PM)* offers American steak-house fare in a classic 19th-century building. **Trading Post (19) ($$)** *(170 John St., Front/South Sts., 646-370-*

3337, www.tradingpostnyc.com, hours: M–W 11AM–1AM, Th–F 11AM–2AM, Sa 5PM–2AM) offers classic yet slightly upscale American cuisine in a cozy setting. Chic, stylish minimalism, sumptuous leather, dark woods, and private nooks provide a calm, intimate venue in the midst of the Wall Street bustle. Wall Street workers are not always big on loyalty to their employers but they are famously loyal to their favorite area restaurants, one of which is **Alfanoose Middle Eastern Cuisine (20) ($)** *(64 Fulton St./Gold and Cliff, 212-528-4669; www.alfanoose. com; hours: daily 11:30AM–9:30PM)*. For a first outing at the restaurant, the falafel—considered some of the best in the city as well as one of the best lunch deals in the Financial District—is a must. **Haru (21) ($$)** *(1 Wall Street Court at Pearl/Beaver Sts., 212-785-6850, www. harusushi.com; hours: M–F 11:30AM–10:30PM, Sa–Su 5PM–10:30PM)* offers classic sushi alongside creative house-specialty rolls at this vibrant spot.

Bars & Nightlife:

The Full Shilling (22) *(160 Pearl St., Wall/Pine Sts., 212-422-3855, www.thefullshilling.com; hours: M–F 11AM–12AM, Sa–Su 11AM–11PM)* is worth going to for the decor alone—a genuine-imported-from-Ireland antique bar that puts any patron in a drinking frame of mind. There is a good selection of beers and comfort food, too.

WHERE TO SHOP

Don't miss Century 21 (23) *(22 Cortlandt St., Broadway/ Church St., 212-227-9092, www.c21stores.com; hours: M–W 7:45AM–9PM, Th–F 7:45AM–9:30PM, Sa 10AM– 9PM, Su 11AM–8PM)*, a department store stuffed with designer clothes for kids and adults at low prices. There's also plenty of shopping at and around the ★SOUTH STREET SEAPORT (24) *(South Street to the East River, Fletcher/Beekman Sts., www. southstreetseaport.com)*, while once a bustling mall, is undergoing a facelift following

TOP PICK!

Hurricane Sandy. While the Pier 17 mall is closed for renovation, many shops along the Seaport remain open for business, like the ever-popular Abercrombie & Fitch, or the more sophisticated Superdry, a chic clothing store out of the U.K. The site still contains many dining options, and some of the best views of the East River and the Brooklyn Bridge. Due to the ever-changing nature of this site, we recommend checking the website for the most up-to-date information.

WHERE TO STAY

The Wall Street Inn (25) (\$\$-\$\$\$) *(9 South William St. at Broad St., 212-747-1500, www.thewallstreetinn.com)* is a small and stylish (if fairly basic) hotel in a neighborhood otherwise given over to large corporate hotels.

BATTERY PARK CITY

❶ *to Chambers St., Rector St.;* ❷❸ *to Chambers St.*

● **SNAPSHOT** ●

Along the Hudson River and west of the financial district is Battery Park City, a mini-metropolis built on landfill that, in typical New York fashion, nestles right next to the most historic part of the city. The Esplanade is one of the star attractions of Battery Park City. Its wide pathways give pedestrians key access to the river. In the midst of this residential neighborhood lies its commercial side: the World Financial Center and Winter Garden.

PLACES TO SEE
Landmarks:

The best thing about Battery Park City (east of the Hudson River from Battery Place to Chambers St.) is its wonderful **Waterfront (26)**, part of a Hudson River Greenway that runs as far north as Harlem. There are spaces to jog, walk, bike, or just sit back and relax, all with amazing views of Jersey City's towers across the water. During warmer months there are always free cul-

tural events *(see www.batteryparkcity.org for details)*. The yachts moored in the **North Cove Yacht Harbor (27)** *(waterfront between Vesey/Liberty Sts.)* are worth ogling. The **Winter Garden (28)** is a glorious 10-story glass atrium with palm trees, food courts, and shopping, plus views of the Hudson and Jersey shores. It is located in the **World Financial Center (28)** plaza *(see page 29)*, which has numerous restaurants and shops, and hosts many (often free) musical and other events *(see www.artsworldfinancialcenter.com for details)*.

Arts & Entertainment:

The ziggurat-shaped **Museum of Jewish Heritage (29)** *(Edmond J. Safra Plaza, 36 Battery Pl. at First Pl., 646-437-4202, www.mjhnyc.org; hours: Su–Tu, Th 10AM–5:45PM; W 10AM–8PM; F, during daylight savings time 10AM–5PM; other F and eve of Jewish holidays 10AM–3PM)*, located in the southern end of Battery Park City, is packed with photographs and objects documenting the past 100 years of Jewish life. The surrounding park and nearby landscaped walkways make for a lovely outside stroll.

Kids:

Battery Park City is one of the most child-friendly places in the city and is so well-designed that adults can enjoy it equally—a rare treat among children's attractions. The big draw here is the beautiful 1.2-mile **Esplanade (30)** that runs along the Hudson River from Chambers Street to Battery Place and offers amazing views of the Statue of Liberty, Ellis Island, and the Jersey City waterfront. Along the Esplanade are numerous small parks for children, adults, and even dogs. For toddlers, the best one is the **Nelson A. Rockefeller Park (31)** *(near Chambers St.)*, which contains the Real World Sculpture Garden, filled with wonderful little bronze sculptures by artist Tom Otterness. There's also a wading fountain to cool off on those hot NYC summer days. The **Robert F. Wagner, Jr. Park (32)** *(southern tip of Battery Park City, south of the Museum of Jewish Heritage)* is also particularly good for young children. It has clean, safe bathrooms, sprinklers in the summer, water tables, and more.

PLACES TO EAT & DRINK
Where to Eat:

Battery Park City is far from the go-to area for eating out though, in recent years, things have gotten slightly better. There are a number of restaurants both inside the **Winter Garden (28)** atrium and lining the plaza outside. If you're strolling around, your best bet is to try a local favorite for take-out—**Terry's Deli (33) ($)** *(41 River Ter. at Chambers St., 212-267-2816; hours: daily 6AM–12AM)* has good, if basic, sandwiches. For one of the best sit-down meals in the area, **Liberty View Restaurant (34) ($$)** *(21 South End Ave. at West Thames St., 212-786-1888, hours: daily: 11:30AM–10PM)* serves several of China's regional cuisines and a view of Lady Liberty herself.

WHERE TO SHOP

The **World Financial Center (28)** has a host of stores and specialty shops to suit all of your needs—from fine cigars to chocolates to designer clothes for men and women.

WHERE TO STAY

The **New York Marriott Downtown (35) ($$$-$$$$)** *(85 West St., Albany/Carlisle Sts., 212-385-4900, www.nycmarriott financial.com)* comes with all the bells and whistles you'd expect, including a fancy restaurant, Internet access in each room, and stunning harbor views.

TRIBECA

1 *to Canal St., Franklin St. or Chambers St.;*
2 3 *to Chambers St.;* **A C E** *to Canal St.*

● SNAPSHOT ●

Tribeca used to be the site of Washington Market, a major distribution center for meat, produce, and dairy products. The warehouses and store-and-loft

buildings here date from the 19th- and early-20th-centuries. After the market moved to the Bronx, the neighborhood was slowly transformed into a residential one. It now offers some of the best eating, drinking, and architecture in the city.

PLACES TO SEE
Landmarks:

Tribeca is home to some of the most flamboyant creations in stone and brick, each vying to outdo the other. **Duane Park (36)** *(Hudson, Duane, and Staple Sts.)* is a delightful triangular pocket, surrounded by cast-iron buildings that were still home to remnants of the city's dairy produce industry until the late 1970s. The **New York Mercantile Exchange Building (37)** *(6 Harrison St., Greenwich/Hudson Sts.)* has a fantastic red brick facade, complete with clock face. Once home to the dairy trade's equivalent of the stock exchange, it has been handsomely restored.

Arts & Entertainment:

Tribeca has also become famous in recent years for resident Robert DeNiro's annual **Tribeca Film Festival** *(www.tribecafilmfestival.org for details)*, held in various neighborhood locations at the end of April. Some think it has become too mainstream in recent years (its attendance has surpassed 300,000 in previous years), but if you're into star-gazing, then this is the place to be each spring. Since its inception in 1994, **apexart (38)** *(291 Church St., White/Walker Sts., 212-431-5270, www.apexart.org; hours: Tu–Sa 11AM–6PM)* has been known for its unpredictable and innovative exhibits. More than 1,200 artists have participated in their wide variety of shows. They also host a number of special programs and events, including artist lectures and round-table discussions. The **Soho Photo Gallery (39)** *(15 White St., West Broadway/Church St., 212-226-8571, www.sohophoto.com: W–Su 1PM–6PM or by appointment)* is one of the numerous galleries that dot Tribeca. Established in 1971 as a non-profit run by a large number of photographers, it offers a dozen or so different shows a year. The Soho name remains, but the gallery relocated to Tribeca in 1979.

Kids:

From October to June the **Tribeca Performing Arts Center (40)** *(199 Chambers St., Greenwich St./West Side Highway, 212-220-1459, www.tribecapac.org)* offers a mixed bag of puppet, theater, and musical shows for children aged 3 and up. If you want to eat out with your children, **Edward's (41) ($)** *(136 West Broadway, Thomas/Duane Sts., 212-233-6436, hours: breakfast M–F 9AM–11AM,*

Sa–Su 9AM–10AM; brunch Sa–Su 10AM–5PM; lunch daily 11AM–5PM; dinner daily 5PM–12AM) offers a handy combination of a Mom- and Dad-friendly hip interior, a child-friendly waitstaff, and a kids' menu that will please the pickiest of wee ones.

PLACES TO EAT & DRINK
Where to Eat:

Tribeca has some of the most famous restaurants in the city. Call in advance for reservations if there's one in which you must dine. For top-end French dining there's **Bouley (42) ($$$$)** *(163 Duane St. at Hudson St., 212-964-2525, www.davidbouley.com; hours: M–Sa 11:30AM–11:30PM)* where Chef David Bouley infuses his flair for tropical flavors with his French grandmother's inspired cooking traditions. Jackets are preferred, but not required. For the restaurant that set the standard for fine Japanese dining, head to **Nobu (43) ($$$)** *(105 Hudson St. at Franklin St., 212-219-0500, www.noburestaurants.com/new-york; hours: M–F 11:45AM–2:15PM, M–Sa 5:45PM–10:15PM, Su 5:45PM–11PM)*. Chef Nobu Matsuhisa's temple to fish also offers some of the best people-watching in the city. For bistro-style Argentinean cooking, which mixes Italian and Spanish culinary influences, visit **Estancia 460 (44) ($$-$$$)** *(460 Greenwich St., Watts/Desbrosses Sts., 212-431-5093, www.estancia460.com, hours: M–Sa 10:30AM–11PM, Su 10:30AM–10PM)*. The name means "ranch house," which is evoked in the upscale rustic decor and familiar, comfortable ambiance. Estancia has been feeding the locals and Tribeca celebs since 1995, and has developed an extended family in the city that flock there for hearty unpretentious fare in a low key and intimate setting. For much more casual lunches and dinners, there's always that reliable old standard **Odeon (45) ($$)** *(145 West Broadway at Duane St., 212-233-0507, www.the odeonrestaurant.com; hours: lunch M–F 11:30AM–5:30PM; dinner daily 5:30PM–12AM; brunch Sa–Su 10AM–4PM)*, a French bistro whose fries and warm mahogany paneling combine for a dining experience as soothing as a warm bath. If you're more into a casual brunch or snack-and-run, there's **Bubby's Tribeca (46) ($)** *(120 Hudson St. at N. Moore St., 212-219-0666, www.bubbys.com; hours: Tu–Su 24 hours, M until 11PM)*, a corner joint that has grown into an institution and is packed on weekends.

Bars & Nightlife:

If you want something a little upmarket, Tribeca is the home of the sophisticated watering hole. **Anotheroom (47)** *(249 W. Broadway, 212-226-1418, hours: Su–M 5PM–2AM, Tu–Sa 5PM–4AM)* has been declared a great date bar. The owners of The Room and The Otheroom stock this, their Tribeca outlet, with a wide selection of Eurobrews and domestic beers that change with the seasons. **Walker's (48)** *(16 N. Moore St. at Varick St., 212-941-0142, www. walkersnyc.com; hours: daily 11AM–4AM)* is a dying breed in this neighborhood—a classic, old-time bar where you can sip pints and chat in a friendly, utterly unpretentious atmosphere. If you get hungry, pop around to the long back room for above-average burgers, fries, and the like.

WHERE TO SHOP

If Deco is your thing, Antiqueria Tribeca (49) *(129 Duane St., West Broadway/Church St., 212-227-7500, www. antiqueria.com; hours: M–Sa 11AM–6PM)* has tons of it, as well as other 20th-century European furnishings and objets d'art, all housed in a landmarked building. Specializing in high-quality antiques from Asia, Abhaya (50) *(145 Hudson St. at Hubert St., 212-431-6931, www.abhayatribeca.com; hours: M–Sa 11AM–6PM)* boasts one of the largest inventories of Asian art and furniture. The store is a treasure trove of sculpture and furnishings from China, Thailand, Laos, and other locations in Asia. Architect Frank Gehry designed the flagship Issey Miyake (51) *(119 Hudson St., Franklin/N. Moore Sts., 212-226-0100, www.tribecaisseymiyake.com; hours: M–Sa, 11AM–7PM, Su 12PM–5PM, seasonal: call ahead to make sure they're open)* store. The space is a stunning showcase for Miyake's sculptural—and pricey—clothing for men and women. At Shoofly (52) *(42 Hudson St., Duane/Thomas Sts., 212-406-*

3270, www.shooflynyc.com; hours: M–Sa 10AM–7PM, Su 12PM–6PM), with its lovely European children's shoes and accessories, you can indulge your parental fantasies about what your little darlings really should look like.

Archipelago (53) *(38 Walker St., Broadway/Church St., 212-334-9460, www.archipelagoinc.com; hours: M–F 9:30AM–5:30PM)* is a must for high-thread-count addicts, thanks to an enormous selection of linens, bedsheets, napkins, and more.

WHERE TO STAY

For most visitors, Tribeca is a playground rather than a place to stay. But if you've got the money, the ultra-sleek 201-room boutique hotel, the **Tribeca Grand (54) ($$$$)** *(2 Avenue of the Americas, White/Walker Sts., 212-519-6600, www.tribecagrand.com),* is not a bad place to rest your head. A bonus of staying here is that the concierge can often get you a table at some of the tightly booked local restaurants. More modestly, there's the 129-room **Cosmopolitan Hotel (55) ($$)** *(95 West Broadway at Chambers St., 888-895-9400, www.cosmohotel.com),* which costs about a third of the price of the Grand and lacks its luxury design, but is one of the city's genuine bargains.

CIVIC CENTER

4 5 6 to Brooklyn Bridge-City Hall;
R to City Hall; **J Z** to Chambers St.

● SNAPSHOT ●

When this area was first built up, it marked the northern edge of the city. When City Hall was being built in 1803, the northern facade of the building was left unfinished because no one thought the city would expand farther north. As was true then, this is where the city government resides. There are a number of imposing, majestic public buildings here. The Woolworth Building was the tallest building in the world from 1913 to 1929, until an uptown rival rose higher.

PLACES TO SEE
Landmarks:

City Hall (56), from which the mayor runs this vast megalopolis, is a white Renaissance creation dating from 1812, set amid lovely gardens with fountains *(Vesey to Chambers Sts., Broadway to Park Row)*. City Hall and the immediate area are closed to the public, but the southern parts of the gardens are open to all. Across from it is the **Municipal Building (57)** *(1 Centre St. opposite Chambers St.)*, with its magnificent colonnade. Upstairs is the public marriage office and chapel, which is both an amusing and genuinely touching place to visit. The most striking building by far is the classic **Woolworth Building (58)** *(233 Broadway, Park Place/Barclay St.)*—a

Gothic masterpiece rising 792 feet, and the tallest building in the world when it opened in 1913. The ★**BROOKLYN BRIDGE (59)** *(entrance near Park Row)* is one of the world's most recognizable and beautiful bridges. This steel and granite span was the longest suspension bridge when it was built in 1883, connecting Manhattan with Brooklyn (which was a separate city before the bridge was built). It makes for a wonderful walk (or ride—bikers on the right, pedestrians on the left) over the East River, offering beautiful views of Manhattan.

TOP PICK!

PLACES TO EAT & DRINK
Where to Eat:

This area caters to a busy brown-bag grabbing workforce during the day. Your best bet is to slip off north and east to Chinatown, or west to Tribeca. If you do want to stay in the area for a quick bite, try **Fulton Street (60)** or **Beekman Street (61)**, where you'll find a variety of small, family-run delicatessens.

WHERE TO SHOP

Over the years, electronics superstore **J&R Music and Computer World** *(1 Park Row, Ann/Beekman Sts., www.jr.com)* expanded to cover virtually all the southern end of Park Row. While they closed the Park Row location, they have opened J&R Express inside Century 21 (23). The store will have a selection of electronics, vinyl, and computer gadgets, plus special musical events on the lower level. *(22 Cortlandt St., Broadway/Church St., 212-227-9092)*.

chapter 2

CHINATOWN
LITTLE ITALY & NOLITA
LOWER EAST SIDE
EAST VILLAGE

CHINATOWN
LITTLE ITALY & NOLITA
LOWER EAST SIDE
EAST VILLAGE

Places to See:

1. Eastern States Buddhist Temple
2. 130 Bowery
3. The Forward Building
4. Columbus Park
5. Museum of the Chinese in the Americas
19. Saint Patrick's Old Cathedral
20. Umberto's Clam House
21. Police Building Apartments
22. Feast of San Gennaro
39. Lower East Side Tenement Museum
40. Eldridge Street Synagogue
41. Cake Shop
42. ABC No Rio
43. Landmark's Sunshine Cinema
60. Nicholas and Elizabeth Stuyvesant Fish House
61. 151 Avenue B
62. New York City Marble Cemetery
63. Grace Church
64. Tompkins Square Park
65. Cooper Union
66. La MaMa E.T.C.
67. St. Mark's-in-the-Bowery Church
68. Bowery Poetry Club
69. KGB
70. Nuyorican Poets Cafe
71. Theater for the New City
72. St. Mark's Place
73. Duo Multicultural Arts Center
74. Michael Mut Gallery
75. First Street Playground

Places to Eat & Drink:

6. Original Chinatown Ice Cream Factory
7. Sheng Wang
8. Fuleen Seafood Restaurant
9. XO Kitchen
10. Joe's Shanghai Restaurant
11. Ping's Seafood
12. Pho Grand
13. Vegetarian Dim Sum House
23. Caffe Napoli

24. Café Gitane
25. Lombardi's
26. Pomodoro
27. Socarrat Paella Bar
28. Café Habana
29. Peasant
30. Public
31. Eileen's Special Cheesecake
32. Mulberry Street Bar
44. Katz's Delicatessen
45. Empanada Mama
46. Congee Village
47. Sauce .
48. il laboratorio del gelato
49. GHOST
50. Marshall Stack
51. The Whiskey Ward
52. The Ten Bells
77. Veselka
78. Two Boots Pizzeria
79. Little India
80. Brick Lane Curry House
81. Frank
82. Caravan of Dreams
83. The Organic Grill
84. Soba-ya
85. Mermaid Inn
86. McSorley's Old Ale House
87. Zum Schneider
88. Boxcar Lounge
89. Angel's Share

Where to Shop:

14. Yunhong Chopsticks Shop
15. Kam Man Food Products
16. Mott Street
17. Ten Ren Tea & Ginseng Co.
18. New Jade Garden Crafts
33. Di Palo's Fine Foods
34. Despaña
35. DöKham
36. Only Hearts
37. Ina Nolita
38. Sigerson Morrison
53. Orchard Street
54. Russ & Daughters
55. Kossar's Bialys
56. Yonah Schimmel Knish Bakery
57. Alife Rivington Club
76. Dinosaur Hill
90. Russian Turkish Baths
91. Duo
92. St. Mark's Bookshop
93. Kiehl's
94. La Sirena
95. Trash and Vaudeville
97. The Strand Bookstore

Where to Stay:

58. Hotel on Rivington
59. Off Soho Suites Hotel
96. East Village Bed & Coffee

CHINATOWN

6 to Canal St.; N R Q to Canal St.;
B D to Grand St.; J Z to Canal-Centre Sts.

• SNAPSHOT •

With its winding alleyways, open air markets, street vendors, Chinese signs, and crowds haggling in Cantonese over future dinner ingredients still swimming in the tank, ★**CHINATOWN** has an old-fashioned and exotic urban atmosphere that makes it one of the favorite destinations for New Yorkers and tourists alike. Over the years Chinatown's boundaries have spread, eating into nearby Little Italy so there's barely a rump of it left. This expansion continues today as immigrants from China, Vietnam, and beyond continue to pour into what is the largest Asian community outside Asia. With its crowded streets and high-speed pace, the atmosphere is always electric in Chinatown.

TOP PICK!

PLACES TO SEE
Landmarks:

Check out the rows of gleaming golden Buddha statues at the **Eastern States Buddhist Temple (1)** *(64 Mott St., Canal/Bayard Sts., 212-966-6229; hours: daily 9AM–6PM).* The **Forward Building (3)** *(173–175 East Broadway, Rutgers/Jefferson Sts.,)* is an intriguing symbol of the continuing growth and vitality of Chinatown. Once the headquarters of a famous Yiddish newspaper, it is now a residential property. In nice weather, the locals play *mah-jongg* (a Chinese game using up to 144 tiles and played with four people) and practice *tai chi* in **Columbus Park (4)** *(Baxter, Bayard, and Mulberry Sts.).*

Arts & Entertainment:

With its amazing cultural diversity, New York hosts many different ethnic and cultural events, but few come close to the extravaganza of the **Chinese New Year**, celebrated every February during a two-week period (the date changes slightly each year) with firecrackers, a huge procession with dancing dragons that snakes in and out of various restaurants, and of course masses of delicious food. It's centered on Mott Street *(call the NYC tourism information line 212-484-1222 for details)* but includes a number of locations. The **Museum of the Chinese in the Americas (MoCA) (5)** *(215 Centre St., Howard/Grand, 212-619-4785, www.mocanyc.org; hours: Tu, W, F–Su 11AM–6PM, Th 11AM–9PM)* is a little-known cultural attraction, but one definitely worth visiting. Housed in a space designed by Maya Lin, it offers not only excellent temporary exhibitions, but also a permanent collection of artifacts, letters, and remarkable photographs documenting the lives of Chinese immigrants to this country.

Kids:

The **Chinese New Year** *(212-484-1222, www.nycvisit. com)*, with its firecrackers and dragon costumes, is fun for older kids if you're here in February, though toddlers might be scared. Kids (and adults!) of all ages will enjoy a treat from the **Original Chinatown Ice Cream Factory (6)** *(65 Bayard St., Mott/Elizabeth Sts., 212-608-4170,* *www.chinatownicecreamfactory.com; hours: daily 11AM–10PM*). They give the popular American dessert an exotic Chinese twist with their range of flavors such as lychee, ginger, red bean, and zen butter. But if you're not feeling that adventurous, they've got all the classics, too!

PLACES TO EAT & DRINK
Where to Eat:

Chinatown has great street food. Vendors selling freshly cooked noodles, pancakes, and other Asian specialties park their carts up and down Canal Street. Any vendor who has a long line of customers waiting is a good bet. The budget traveler can eat very well here, but remember to bring cash: many restaurants do not accept credit cards. Although you can never choose wrong simply by looking in the windows to find a packed house, some reliable standards are these: **Sheng Wang (7) ($)** *(27 Eldridge St., near Canal, 212-925-0805; hours: daily 11AM–10PM)* serves soups—with meats from the tame to the intestinal—loaded with handmade noodles. Fresh fish swimming in their tanks will greet you at **Fuleen Seafood Restaurant (8) ($$)** *(11 Division St., near Bowery, 212-941-6888, hours: daily 11AM–11:30PM).* **XO Kitchen (9) ($)** *(148 Hester St., Bowery/Elizabeth St., 212-965-8645, www.xokitchen.com; cash only; hours: Su–Th 8AM–11PM, F–Sa 8AM–11:30PM)* specializes in the cuisine of Hong Kong. The legendary dumplings at **Joe's Shanghai Restaurant (10) ($–$$)** *(9 Pell St., Mott/Bowery Sts., 212-233-8888, cash only, www.joeshanghairestaurants.com; hours: daily 11AM–11PM)* explain the long line of people usually waiting to get in. But it's worth the wait. Just make sure to first take a nibble into the dumpling, and then "slurp" the soup out to avoid burning your mouth! Fresh seafood and a slightly more upscale atmosphere are the draws of **Ping's Seafood (11) ($$)** *(22 Mott St., Mosco/Pell Sts., 212-602-9988, www.pings nyc.com; hours: M–F 10AM–11PM, Sa–Su 9AM–11PM)*—a Chinatown favorite. Or, get in on the city's love affair with Vietnamese pho at **Pho Grand (12) ($)** *(277 Grand St. at Forsyth, 212-965-5366, www.phograndny.com; hours: daily 10:30AM–11PM)*. The setting is minimal, but the menu is huge at the **Vegetarian Dim Sum House (13) ($)** *(24 Pell St., Mott/Bowery Sts., 212-577-7176, www. vegetariandimsum.com; hours: daily 10:30AM–10:30PM)*.

WHERE TO SHOP

Pick up a genuine pair of chopsticks from Yunhong Chopsticks Shop (14) *(50 Mott St., at Bayard St., 212-566-8828, www.happychopsticks.com; hours: daily 10:30AM–8:30PM)*. Chinatown is a popular destination for bargain hunters. **Canal Street**, especially, is lined with shops selling cheap knockoff designer watches and gold jewelry. Stop in at Kam Man Food Products (15) *(200 Canal St. at Mulberry St., 212-571-0330, www.newkamman.com, hours: daily 9AM–8:30PM)* for everything from dried jellyfish to cookware. Mott Street (16) is a good place to pick up cheap souvenirs like Chinese children's pajamas, beaded slippers, and bits of jade. For interesting teas, stop in at the Ten Ren Tea & Ginseng Co. (17) *(75 Mott St., Canal/Bayard Sts., 212-349-2286, www.tenrenusa. com; hours: daily 11AM–8PM)*. You'll find Eastern teapots, flowerpots, and more at the New Jade Garden Crafts (18) *(76 Mulberry St., Canal/Bayard Sts., 212-587-5685; hours: daily 10AM–7PM)*.

● SNAPSHOT ●

Since most of the immigrants (and their descendants) who once lived on or around Mulberry Street have moved out to other Italian neighborhoods or the 'burbs, the enclave of Little Italy is just a shadow of its former self. The crowds still come, however, to enjoy the restaurants, cafés, groceries, and the week-long Feast of San Gennaro every September. Nolita (North of Little Italy) is a relatively new neighborhood, home to one-of-a-kind boutiques for the young and fashionable.

PLACES TO SEE
Landmarks:

Probably the most beautiful spot in the neighborhood is **Saint Patrick's Old Cathedral (19)** *(263 Mulberry St., Houston/Prince Sts., 212-226-8075, www.oldcathedral. org; rectory hours M–F 8AM–5PM)*. Built in 1809–1815 in a Gothic Revival style, it's the oldest Catholic Church in the city. **Umberto's Clam House (20)** *(132 Mulberry St. Grand/Hester, 212-431-7545, www.umbertosclamhouse. com; hours: daily 11AM–1AM)*, a very different historic landmark, is where Joey Gallo, a famous Mafioso, was shot to death in 1972. The **Police Building Apartments (21)** *(240 Centre St., Grand/Broome Sts.)*, built in 1905–1909, is a handsome Edwardian structure with a huge dome.

The police department vacated it in 1973, and 10 years later it was converted into cooperative apartments. Walk over to **130 Bowery (2)** *(130 Bowery, Broome/Grand Sts.)*, designed by the famous New York architecture firm, McKim, Mead & White, in 1893. Its marble Corinthian columns and soaring ceilings won it landmark status in 1966. Previously the Bowery Savings Bank **130 Bowery (2)** is now home to Capitale, a restaurant and event space.

Arts & Entertainment:

Little Italy's pleasures lie mostly in strolling around its old tenement-lined streets, absorbing its plentiful street life and, of course, sampling its gastronomic delights. But every September Little Italy is host to the **Feast of San Gennaro (22)** *(Mulberry St., Canal/Houston Sts., 212-768-9320, www.sangennaro.org)*, a huge tourist attraction with endless food vendors lining the streets, and a Ferris wheel and other sideshow pleasures imported. Many New Yorkers avoid it like the plague, considering its charms to have vanished long ago, but there's no denying that at night, with the streets all lit up, it can be a romantic sight.

Kids:

Italy is famous for its child-indulging culture, and kids are welcome in most of Little Italy's restaurants, though it's quite an urban area and otherwise not of the greatest interest to most young ones. If you're here in September, the **Feast of San Gennaro (22)** *(see page 46)* will probably hold their attention most. **Caffe Napoli (23)**

(191 Hester St. at Mulberry St., 212-226-8705; hours: daily 9AM–1AM) lets you take your time demolishing your plate of pasta and offers children's portions as well.

PLACES TO EAT & DRINK
Where to Eat:

Café Gitane (24) ($) *(242 Mott St., Houston/Prince Sts., 212-334-9552; hours: Su–Th 8:30AM–12AM, F–Sa 8:30AM–12:30AM)*, right across the street from St. Patrick's, is a good place to sit, sip mint tea, nibble reasonably priced Moroccan specialties, and gaze on the church with its peaceful, tree-shaded cemetery. **Lombardi's (25) ($)** *(32 Spring St., Mott/Mulberry Sts., 212-941-7994, cash only, www.first pizza.com; hours: Su–Th 11:30AM–11PM, F–Sa 11:30AM–12AM)* offers great New York pizza pies (no slices) in a turn-of-the-century restaurant. There's no shortage of pizza places in Little Italy. Try **Pomodoro (26) ($)** *(51 Spring St.,*

*at Mulberry St., 212-966-9229, www.pomodoropizza
ny.com; hours: M–Sa 11AM–11:45PM, Su 11AM–9PM)*
for the best vodka pizza you've ever tasted. For a taste
of Spain, check out **Socarrat Paella Bar (27) ($$)** *(284
Mulberry St. at E. Houston, 212-219-0101, www.
socarratnolita.com; hours: brunch Sa–Su 12PM–4PM, din-
ner Su–Th 5PM–11PM, F–Sa 5PM–11:30PM).* A neigh-
borhood favorite since it first opened in 1997, **Café
Habana (28) ($)** *(17 Prince St., at Elizabeth, 212-625-
2001; www.cafehabana.com; hours: daily 9AM–12AM)* is
a veritable Nolita institution. Their grilled corn on the
cob—done up in Mexican style—will make your taste
buds sing. It's coated in the perfect amount of lime,
chili powder, and cheese. Their Cuban sandwich is also
an award winner. **Peasant (29) ($$-$$$)** *(194 Elizabeth
St., Prince/Spring Sts., 212-965-9511; www.peasantnyc.
com; hours: Tu–Th 6PM–11PM, F–Sa 6PM–11PM, Su
6PM–10PM)* provides rustic Italian cuisine served in a
dim, romantic interior. **Public (30) ($$$)** *(210 Elizabeth
St., Prince/Spring Sts., 212-343-7011; www.public-nyc.
com; hours: M–Th 6PM–11PM with bar open to 1AM; F–
Sa 6PM–12AM with bar open to 2AM; Su 6PM–10:30PM
with bar open to 1AM; brunch Sa–Su 11AM–3:30PM)*—
and the attached 20-seat wine bar—offer global cuisine
with uncommon ingredients. Grab a mini cheesecake
to go—park bench picnic, anybody?—from **Eileen's
Special Cheesecake (31) ($)** *(17 Cleveland Pl. at the cor-
ner of Kenmare/Centre Sts., 212-966-5585; www.eileens
cheesecake.com; hours: M–F 9AM–9PM, Sa–Su 10AM–7PM).*

Bars & Nightlife:

If you want to feel like a star in your very own *Mean Streets*, **Mulberry Street Bar (32)** (formerly **Mare Chiaro**) (*176 Mulberry St., Broome/Grand Sts., 212-226-9345, cash only; hours: M–Sa 11AM–4AM, Su 12PM–4AM*)—an old dark dive complete with phone booth, photos of the owner posing with what was then a very down-town Madonna—will fit the bill. Order a cheap beer and play some Sinatra on the jukebox.

WHERE TO SHOP

Go to **Di Palo's Fine Foods (33)** (*200 Grand St. at Mott St., 212-226-1033; www.dipaloselects.com; hours: M–Sa 9AM–6:30PM, Su 9AM–4PM*) to stock up on Italian ingredients (or get picnic-worthy sandwiches), or **Despaña (34)** (*408 Broome St., Lafayette/Cleveland, 212-219-5050, www.despananyc.com; M–F 10AM–7PM, Sa 11AM–7PM, Su 11AM–6PM*) for Spanish tapas and other treats. **DöKham (35)** (*51 Prince St., Mott/Mulberry Sts., 212-996-2404; www.dokhamny.com; hours: daily 10AM–8PM*), a Tibetan shop, has silk stoles, striking silver jewelry,  and stunning fur-lined Tibetan hats. The boutique shop **Only Hearts (36)** (*230 Mott St., Prince/Spring Sts., 212-431-3694, www.onlyhearts.com; hours: M–Sa 11:30AM–7:30PM, Su 11:30AM–6:30PM*), has much more to offer than just hearts—from lingerie to dresses you'll find unique and fashionable items to add to your wardrobe. If you're a fashionista on a budget, Ina Nolita (37) *(21 Prince St., Elizabeth/Mott Sts., 212-334-9048, www.inanyc.com; hours: M–Sa 12PM–8PM, Su 12PM–7PM)* is a designer consignment shop. If you have more cash to spare, try Sigerson Morrison (38) *(28 Prince St., Elizabeth/Mott Sts., 212-219-3893, www.siger sonmorrison.com; hours: M–Sa 11AM–7PM, Su 12PM–6PM)* for seriously fashion-forward footwear.

LOWER EAST SIDE

F *to Delancey St. or Second Ave.;*
J Z *to Essex St.*

● SNAPSHOT ●

In the early years of the 20th century, the Lower East Side was the most densely populated area in the world. Primarily a Jewish neighborhood, its tenements were also crammed with immigrants from Eastern Europe, Italy, Germany, and Ireland, who worked in sweatshops and filled the streets with the neigh-  borhood's distinctive pushcarts. Although the living conditions, as revealed by the muckraking journalist, Jacob A. Riis, in his book *How the Other Half Lives*, were often grim, the denizens of the Lower East Side gave back much to America. George Gershwin, Ira Gershwin, the Marx Brothers, Al Smith, and many others were born or grew up here. In the 1960s, the ethnic makeup of the Lower East Side began to change as the older immigrant groups moved out and Hispanics began to move in. Drawn by cheap rents, many artists, musicians, and writers joined the mélange.

PLACES TO SEE

Landmarks:

Give the area—and NYC—context with a visit to the **Lower East Side Tenement Museum (39)** *(103 Orchard St., Broome/Delancey Sts., 212-982-8420, www. tenement.org; hours: Visitor Center open F–W 10AM–6:30PM Th 10AM–8:30PM except for Thanksgiving, Christmas Day, and New Year's Day).* The exhibits in this old tenement building recapture the daily life of the families that once lived here. The museum can only be seen by guided tour, so book ahead. Many of the area's synagogues have now been converted into other uses or are in extreme disrepair, but the **Eldridge Street Synagogue (40)** *(12 Eldridge St., Canal/Division Sts., 212-219-0302, www.eldridge street.org; hours: open to the public Su–Th 10AM–5PM, F 10AM–3PM),* the oldest, is still in use and offers guided tours. Take note of its elaborate Moorish interiors and new stained-glass window by artist Kiki Smith. The **New Museum** *(235 Bowery, 212-219-1222, www.newmuseum. org; hours: Tu–Su 11AM–6PM, Th til 9PM)* is exclusively dedicated to presenting contemporary art from around the world.

Arts & Entertainment:

The Village Voice, Time Out, and *The New York Press* all provide listings for music around town. The specialty of **Cake Shop (41)** *(152 Ludlow St., Rivington/ Stanton Sts., 212-253-0036, www.cake-shop.com)* is independent music and comforting baked goods; an excellent combo. For poetry readings, **ABC No Rio (42)** *(156 Rivington St., Clinton/Suffolk Sts., 212-254-3697,* *www.abcnorio.org*) offers a budget-friendly open mic series every Sunday at 3PM. In the mood for a movie? **Landmark's Sunshine Cinema (43)** *(143 E. Houston St., First/Second Aves., 212-260-7289, www.landmark theatres.com)*, housed in what once was a Yiddish vaudeville theater, has independent art films and great NYC cinephile crowds.

Kids:

The Lower East Side is a dense urban neighborhood full of fascinating history and other adult attractions. The neighborhood's cultural history comes alive through food at **Katz's Delicatessen (44) ($)** *(205 E. Houston St. at Ludlow St., 212-254-2246, www.katzsdelicatessen.com; hours: Su 8AM–10:45PM, M–W, Su 8AM–10:45PM, Th–Sa 8AM–2:45AM)*, **Yonah Schimmel Knish Bakery (56)** *(137 E. Houston St., Forsyth/Eldridge Sts., 212-477-2858, www. knishery.com; hours: M–Th 9AM–7PM, F–Su 9AM–11PM)*, and **Kossar's Bialys (55)** *(367 Grand St., Essex/Norfolk Sts., 212-473-4810, www.kossarsbialys.com; hours: M–Th, Su 9AM–7PM, F–Sa 9AM–9PM)*. The **Tenement Museum (39)** *(see page 52)* has tours designed for kids ages 5 and older. The best playgrounds in the vicinity can be found in the East Village *(see page 61)*, though you'll come across numerous **community gardens** as you stroll around the Lower East Side—most of which are usually pretty child-friendly.

PLACES TO EAT & DRINK
Where to Eat:

Katz's Delicatessen (44) ($) *(205 E. Houston St. at Ludlow St., 212-254-2246, www.katzsdelicatessen.com; hours: M–W, Su 8AM–10:45PM, Th–Sa 8AM–2:45AM)*—grab a hot dog or a pastrami sandwich at this New York institution. **Empanada Mama (45) ($)** *(189 E. Houston St. at Orchard St., 212-673-0300, empmamanyc.com; hours: daily 24 hours)* offers up empanadas, arepas, and more in a cozy, colorful setting. The neon-highlighted interior of **Congee Village (46) ($)** *(100 Allen St. at Delancey, 212-941-1818; www.congeevillagerestaurants.com; hours: Su–Th 10:30AM–12:30AM, F–Sa 10:30AM–2AM)* is a treat for the eyes but the Cantonese cuisine is even better. Great for groups. **Sauce (47) ($)** *(78 Rivington St. at Allen St., 212-420-7700, www.saucerestaurant.com; hours: M–F 5PM–12AM, Sa 11AM–1AM, Su 11AM–12AM)* is the recently-opened chic Italian brainchild of New York restaurateur Frank Prisinzano, owner of the East Village restaurant **Frank (81)** and its adjacent wine bar Vera. Sauce features a more casual flair, and diners can see their charcuterie carved and prepared in the open kitchen. Other specialties include house-made pasta, fancy cheeses, and meatballs. Cap a visit to the lower east side with one of the day's 20 flavors of gelato or sorbet at **il laboratorio del gelato (48) ($)** *(188 Ludlow St. at Houston, 212-343-9922; www. laboratoriodelgelato.com; hours: M–Th 7:30AM–10PM, F 7:30AM–12AM, Sa 10AM–12AM, Su 10AM–10PM)*.

Bars & Nightlife:

GHOST (49) (*132 Eldridge St., Ste. A, Delancey/Broome Sts., 212-775-8390, www.ghostoneldridge.com; hours: M–Th 4PM–12AM, F 4PM–1AM, Sa 12PM–1AM, Su 12PM–12AM*) offers cocktails served alongside art exhibits. With some of the most beer-knowledgeable bartenders in the area—and a not-loud atmosphere that makes for a great place to sit and chat—**Marshall Stack (50)** (*66 Rivington St. at Eldridge St., 212-228-4667; hours: M–W 4PM–2AM, Th–F 4PM–4AM, Sa 1PM–4AM, Su 1PM–2AM*) could become your favorite local bar while you're in town. Worry not, wine and whiskey lovers: the menu has you covered, too. **The Whiskey Ward (51)** (*121 Essex St., Rivington/Delancey Sts., 212-477-2988, www.the whiskeyward.com; hours: M–Sa 5PM–4AM, Su 6PM–4AM*) is a Lower East Side mainstay that boasts an absurdly long list of whiskeys, bourbons, and ryes, as well as a delicious cocktail list. Boisterous on the weekends and mellow on the weekdays, this modern-day saloon offers a dark, warm sanctuary at the end of a long day. **The Ten Bells (52)** (*247 Broome St., Ludlow/Orchard Sts., 212-228-4450; hours: M–F 5PM–2AM, Sa–Su 3PM–2AM*) features an extensive wine list, delicious small plates, and plenty of seating for a mid-shopping break.

WHERE TO SHOP

Shopping in the Lower East Side is a rich cultural experience. The vendors on Orchard Street (53) may now speak Spanish instead of Yiddish, but they offer great bargains in clothing, shoes, and luggage. And if you're hungry, there's Russ & Daughters (54) (*179 East Houston*

St., Allen/Orchard Sts., 212-475-4880, www.russand *daughters.com; hours: M–F 8AM–8PM, Sa 8AM–7PM,* *Su 8AM–5:30PM)* for lox and other smoked fish. They recently opened a café on 127 Orchard St. which offers their renowned delicacies. Visit Kossar's Bialys (55) *(367 Grand St., Essex/Norfolk Sts., 212-473-4810, www.kossarsbialys.com; hours: daily 6AM–8PM)* for fresh-baked bialys and bagels, and don't miss Yonah Schimmel Knish Bakery (56) *(137 E. Houston St., Forsyth/Eldridge Sts., 212-477-2858, www.knishery.com; hours: daily 9AM–8PM)* for a hot knish. If you want to get that oh-so-cool Lower East Side look, head to Alife Rivington Club (57) *(158 Rivington St., Suffolk/Clinton Sts., 212-432-7200, www.alifenewyork.com; hours: M–Sa 12PM–7PM, Su 12PM–6PM)*. Of course, fashion comes with a hefty price tag.

WHERE TO STAY

A hotel in the Lower East Side? Years ago the idea would have seemed absurd. But it's a sign of the times that the luxurious Hotel on Rivington (58) ($$$$) *(107 Rivington St., Essex/Ludlow Sts., 212-475-2600, www.hotelon rivington.com)* not only exists, but is also an ultra-ritzy glass-enveloped 21-story tower complete with every amenity you can think of. The rooftop bar offers stunning views. Also on Rivington, but a lot less splashy, is Off Soho Suites Hotel (59) ($-$$$) *(11 Rivington St., Bowery/Chrystie St., 800-633-7646, www.offsoho.com)*, a strangely corporate name for what is a basic, good-value, no-nonsense place to stay.

6 *to Astor Place;* **N R** *to 8th St.-NYU;*
B D F M *to Broadway-Lafayette St.*

• **SNAPSHOT** •

The East Village tends to blur, in many people's minds, with the Lower East Side—they're both equal parts grungy and hip. But there are differences between the two neighborhoods, and for the purposes of this guide the East Village is considered to begin north of Houston Street, and the Lower East Side south of it. Both the East Village and the Lower East Side have taken on new, post-immigrant lives as hotbeds for the arts in the years since WWII. They became the places where artists, musicians, and writers congregated after Greenwich Village began its inexorable climb to bourgeois respectability and astronomical real estate prices. The Beat generation found succor here in the '50s and '60s; later, punk rock was nurtured at the infamous CBGB's club on the Bowery, and artists such as Keith Haring and Jeff Koons turned the East Village into the nation's hippest artistic center. Then in the '70s heroin hit the neighborhood badly. In the '80s real estate developers began to see promise in the area and the term "East Village" became a relatively new and distinct appellation for the neighborhood. The old East Village did not go quietly into the night—there were riots in 1988 and 1995 as large numbers of squatters were evicted from its streets and parks, but its face inevitably began to change into what it is today, still an exciting, astonishingly multicultural human bazaar, but one with coffee shops—including yes, Starbucks—delis, restaurants, and boutiques on every corner. Changed though it is, it remains one of the most vital parts of the city, and a stroll down its highly charged streets is mandatory for any pedestrian explorer of Manhattan.

PLACES TO SEE
Landmarks:
In the early 19th century the East Village was a wealthy middle-class neighborhood full of grand houses before the great waves of immigrants arrived in the late 19th century, followed in the 1950s by the raffish artists and other free spirits who turned it into New York's great Bohemia. Vestiges of this grand past can still be found amid tenement buildings, such as the **Nicholas and Elizabeth Stuyvesant Fish House (60)** *(21 Stuyvesant St., E. Ninth/E. 10th Sts.)*. Built in the Federal style in 1803 for the great-grandson of the last Dutch general of what was then New Amsterdam, it's one of the earliest residential buildings in the city. Its generous proportions and handsome brick facade make a stark contrast with the cramped dwellings that subsequent residents of the neighborhood usually endured. It's now owned by nearby Cooper Union and is the official residence of its president. As well as tenement buildings, the East Village has a number of lovely brick and brownstone row houses dating from the mid-19th century. For a particularly fine example, check out **151 Avenue B (61)** *(E. Ninth/E. 10th Sts.)*, also known as "Bird's House," as its ground floor was home to saxophonist Charlie Parker from 1950 to 1954. The **New**

York City Marble Cemetery (62) *(52-74 E. Second St., First/ Second Aves., 917-780-2893, www.nycmc.org; entrance may be arranged by special appointment)* is another survivor of the neighborhood's solid past. Unless you gain entry on one of the occasional public tours, you can only get a tantalizing peek through the gate at this charming cemetery where some of New York's most illustrious citizens are buried, including the original inhabitant of the Stuyvesant Fish House. Grace Church (63) *(802 Broadway at E. 10th St., 212-254-2000, www.gracechurchnyc.org)* is one of the most beautiful churches in the city—a delicate Gothic Revival creation with a particularly lovely steeple, and surrounding gardens. It's open to the public and offers concerts. The East Village's main public space is Tompkins Square Park (64) *(E. Seventh to E. 10th Sts., Aves. A/B, www.nycgovparks.org)*. Like so many other parks in the city, this one has seen a major and controversial overhaul in recent years that resulted in the eviction of a large number of homeless people and subsequent radical re-landscaping to avoid those hidden pockets where insalubrious elements might dwell. With the rampant gentrification of recent years it's now a safe and family-friendly environment, though this being the East Village, there's still plenty of interesting people-watching to do.

Arts & Entertainment:

Legend has it that there are denizens of the East Village who never go above 14th Street. Their feeling is: why bother? If they want history, they can always go to Cooper Union (65) *(30 Cooper Square, E. Eighth St./Fourth Ave., 212-353-4100, www.cooper.edu)*, New York's first free nonsectarian college, where Abraham Lincoln gave his famous "Right makes might" speech. If they want drama, **La MaMa E.T.C. (66)** *(74A E. Fourth St., Bowery/ Second Ave., 212-254-6468, www.lamama.org)* offers edgier alternatives to Broadway. They specifically try to support and nourish artists of all nations and cultures. If literature is their love, the poetry readings at **St. Mark's-in-the-Bowery Church (67)** *(131 E. 10th St. at Second Ave., 212-674-6377, stmarksbowery.org)*, the **Bowery Poetry Club (68)** *(308 Bowery, Bleecker/Houston Sts., 212-614-0505, www.bowerypoetry.com)*, **KGB (69)** *(85 E. Fourth St., Second/Third Aves., 212-505-3360, www.kgbbar. com)* and the **Nuyorican Poets Cafe (70)** *(236 E. Third St., Aves. B/C, 212-780-9386, www.nuyorican.org)* beckon. The **Theater for the New City (71)** *(155 First Avenue, 9th/10th Sts., 212-254-1109, www.theaterforthenewcity. net)* produces 30-40 new American plays per year, of which about ten are by emerging, young playwrights. But that barely scratches the surface of all the East Village has to offer. It has the liveliest street life in the city. Walk down **St. Mark's Place (72)** to see a mix of art students, slackers, hipsters, rock musicians, and rev-olutionaries. You may be inspired to get some ink, or a piercing, in one of the tattoo parlors that line the street. There's a thriving art scene with small galleries dotting the area. **Duo Multicultural Arts Center (73)** *(62 E. 4th St., Bowery/2nd Ave., 212-598-4320, www.duotheater. org)* gives visitors a chance to wander through a world's worth of cultures and arts. All inside: works in theater, film, dance, music, and fine arts. Or for experimental photographers, painters, and mixed-media artists, visit the **Michael Mut Gallery (74)** *(97 Avenue C, 6th/7th Sts.,*

917-691-8390, www.mmprojectspace.com; hours vary by exhibit). The gallery focuses on giving artists "a platform for contemplation on current events."

Kids:

The **First Street Playground (75)** *(Houston and E. First St., First/Second Aves.)* has plenty of shade and inventive climbing frames for younger children. **Tompkins Square Park (64)** *(E. Seventh to E. 10th Sts., Aves. A/B)* has no less than three separate and excellent playgrounds, complete with climbing frames, and all are safely enclosed from the street. There are also numerous highly funky and original children's stores around here. One of the best is **Dinosaur Hill (76)** *(306 E. Ninth St., First/Second Aves., 212-473-5850, www.dinosaurhill. com; hours: daily 11AM–7PM)*, which has a wonderful selection of wooden toys, puppets, windup toys, and other classics.

PLACES TO EAT & DRINK
Where to Eat:

Italian, Indian, Eastern European, Korean, Latin American, Mexican, even American—if you're looking for a great bargain meal, the East Village is the place to go. No matter what cuisine or ambience you're in the mood for, the East Village will probably have a restaurant to suit both your cravings and your pocket. On a cold winter's day, order a piping hot bowl of borscht at **Veselka (77)** **($)** *(144 Second Ave. at E. Ninth St., 212-228-9682, www.veselka.com; hours: daily 24 hours)*, a gussied-up Ukrainian 24-hour-coffee shop (dig those crazy murals of East Village types on the walls).

Hipsters, college students, and families crowd into **Two Boots Pizzeria (78) ($)** *(42 Ave. A at 3rd St., 212-254-1919, www.twoboots.com: Su–Tu 11:30AM–11PM, W–Th 11:30AM–12AM, F–Sa 11:30AM–2AM)* for its pizzas and funky vibe. East Sixth Street between Second and First avenues (and now extending a tad eastward to Ave. A) is known as **Little India (79)**. **Brick Lane Curry House (80) ($-$$)** *(99 Second Ave., 5th/6th Sts., 212-979-8787, www.bricklanecurryhouse.com: Su–Th 1PM–11PM, F–Sa 1PM–1AM)* is a British-style curry shop known for spicy dishes. Come early if you don't want to wait in line at **Frank (81) ($)** *(88 Second Ave., E. Fifth/E. Sixth Sts., 212-420-0106, www.frankrestaurant.com; hours: Su 10:30AM–1AM, M–Th 10:30AM–1AM, F–Sa 10:30AM–2AM)*, a lively, homey restaurant that serves up heaping plates of Italian favorites. Delicious organic, vegan, world-fusion cuisine awaits you at **Caravan of Dreams (82) ($$)** *(405 E. 6th St., 1st Ave/Ave A, 212-254-1613, www.caravan ofdreams.net; hours: Su–F 11AM–11PM, Sa 11AM–12AM)*. There's live music most every night. Young hipsters love **The Organic Grill (83) ($$)** *(123 First Ave., E. Seventh St./ St. Marks Pl., 212-477-7177, www.theorganicgrill.com; hours: daily 12PM–10PM)* for its consistently delicious vegan-oriented menu that stresses organic, local ingredients. If you have a yen for Japanese food, **Soba-ya (84) ($$)** *(229 E. 9th St., Second/Third Aves., 212-533-6966, www.sobaya-nyc.com; hours: lunch M–F 12PM–3:30PM, Sa–Su 12PM–3:50PM, dinner Su–Th 5:30PM–10:30PM F–Sa to 11PM)* serves up satisfying bowls of the noodles known as udon and a wide selection of Japanese beer. And if all this foreign food leaves you with a craving for Americana, get good old New England fish shack classics at the **Mermaid Inn (85) ($$)** *(96 Second Ave., E. Fifth/E. Sixth Sts., 212-674-5870, www.themermaidnyc.com; hours: M 5PM–10PM, Tu–F 5PM–11PM, Sa 4PM–11PM, Su 4PM–11PM).*

Bars & Nightlife:

The East Village has a hopping bar scene. Have a beer at the fabled **McSorley's Old Ale House (86)** *(15 E. Seventh St., Second/Third Aves., 212-473-9148, www.mcsorleysnew york.com; hours: M–Sa 11AM–1AM, Su 1PM–1AM).* Opened in 1854, this little piece of old New York has sawdust on the floors, old newspaper clippings on the wall, and its own ale. **Zum Schneider (87)** *(107 Ave. C at E. Seventh St., 212-598-1098, www.zumschneider.com; hours: M–Th 5PM–2AM, F 4PM–4AM, Sa 1PM–4AM, Su 1PM–12AM)* is a great place for German beer, with 12 kinds on tap. **Boxcar Lounge (88)** *(168 Ave. B, E. 10th/E. 11th Sts., 212-473-2830, www.boxcarlounge.com; hours: M–Th, 6PM–4AM, F 4PM–4AM, Sa–Su 6PM–4AM)* offers a cozy atmosphere and ivied patio, as well as a killer happy hour. If you're in the mood for something more sophisticated, walk up the stairs of **8 Stuyvesant St.** *(St. Marks Pl./E. Ninth St.)* and through the **Village Yokocho** Japanese restaurant into the tiny **Angel's Share (89)** *(212-777-5415; hours: Su–W 6PM–1:30AM, Th 6PM–2AM, F–Sa 6PM–2:30AM).* Collapse into one of the cozy armchairs and order a dry martini. Your Japanese waiter will mix it for you at your table. Enjoy it while gazing out the windows at Astor Place and the crowds below.

WHERE TO SHOP

St. Mark's Place (72) *(Eighth St., Third Ave./Ave. A)* is a jumble of CD stores, head shops, comic book shops, T-shirt and cheap jewelry stands, cafés and bars, and is crowded with young 20-somethings and NYU students day and night. East of First Avenue, **Avenues A, B,** and the slowly-emerging **C** have an artier, edgier vibe. Alphabet City—as the avenues from A on back are known—was, at one time, quite a rough neighborhood. Now, hip shops, beauty parlors, and restaurants line many of the blocks. **East Seventh Street** and **Stuyvesant Street** (a one-block gem between St. Mark's Place on Third Avenue and East Ninth Street) are beautiful tree-shaded, brownstone-lined streets where many off-beat clothing and jewelry designers have set up shop. If it's all too much for you, take time for a *shvitz* (Yiddish for steam bath) at the Russian Turkish Baths (90) *(268 E. 10th St., First Ave./Ave. A, 212-674-9250, www. russianturkishbaths.com; hours: M–Tu coed 12PM–10PM; W women only 10AM–2PM, coed 2PM–10PM; Th men only 12PM–5PM, coed 5PM–10PM; F coed 12PM–10PM; Sa coed 9AM–10PM; Su men only 8AM–2PM, coed 2PM–10PM, shorts must be worn during coed hours).* It's a perfect way to take a time-trip back to the days when the streets were packed with immigrants, Second Avenue was the Broadway of the Yiddish theater scene, and tenement apartments had a bathtub in the kitchen. For clothes by emerging designers and beautiful vintage pieces, head straight to Duo (91) *(337 E. Ninth St. near First Ave., 212-777-7044; www.duonyc. com; hours: daily 1PM–8:30PM).* For the book lover, The Strand Bookstore (97) *(828 Broadway, corner of E. 12th St., 212-473-1452, www.strandbooks.com; hours: M–Sa*

9:30AM–10:30PM, Su 11:00AM–10:30PM, *rare book room closes daily at 6:15PM*) is essential browsing. The store's eighteen miles of books cover just about every topic, and the prices are deeply discounted. Make sure to check out the Rare Book Room on the top floor for rare first editions and signed books. Head to St. Mark's Bookshop (92) *(31 Third Ave., at E. Ninth St., 212-260-7853, www.stmarks bookshop.com; hours: M–Sa 11AM–11PM, Su 12PM–11PM)* for photography books, literary journals, and tons of trendy literati ambience. Kiehl's (93) *(109 Third Ave., E.13th/E.14th Sts., 212-677-3171, www.kiehls.com; hours: M–Sa 10AM–8PM, Su 11AM–6PM)*, which started blending its distinctive lotions and shampoos mid-19th century, is internationally-known now, but the high-ceilinged emporium is still the place to go to be served by pleasant, knowledgeable salespeople in their pristine lab coats. The vibrant Mexican folk art for sale at La Sirena (94) *(27 E. 3rd St., 2nd Ave./Bowery, 212-780-9113, www.la sirenanyc.com; daily 12PM–7PM)* may jump in the souvenir line ahead of that NYC snow globe you were considering. Founded in the 1970s, Trash and Vaudeville (95) *(4 St. Mark's Pl. at Cooper Sq., 212-982-3590, www.trashandvaudeville.com, hours: M–Th 12PM–8PM, F 11:30AM–8:30PM, Sa 11:30AM–9PM, Su 1PM–7:30PM)* is full of rock and punk fashions.

WHERE TO STAY

The East Village Bed & Coffee (96) ($-$$) *(110 Ave. C, E. Seventh/E. Eighth Sts., 917-816-0071, www.bedand coffee.com)* is a walk-up brownstone with chic rooms, a private garden and loaner bicycles for guests, plus a live-in hostess. A real New York gem.

chapter 3

NOHO
SOHO
GREENWICH VILLAGE
UNION SQUARE

NoHo
SoHo
Greenwich Village
Union Square

Places to See:

Places to Eat & Drink:

NOHO

● SNAPSHOT ●

In the 1970s, this area of warehouses north of Houston Street (hence its acronym NoHo for "North of Houston Street") began to draw artists escaping from the escalating rents of neighboring Soho. In 1976, the neighborhood was rezoned so that artists could both live and work there. Today, NoHo is a small, but bustling, neighborhood known as much for its popular restaurants and shopping as its arts scene.

PLACES TO SEE
Landmarks:

The **Noho Historic District** *(roughly E. Houston St. to Astor Pl., Broadway/Bowery)* received its Landmarks designation in 1999. It contains some astonishing buildings in a remarkable variety of styles and materials. The **Bayard-Condict Building (1)** *(65-69 Bleecker St., Broadway/Lafayette St.)* is an early skyscraper (13 stories!) and the only Louis Sullivan building in New York. Its lovely white terra-cotta facade has beautifully organic, ornate details. The **Bond Street Savings Bank (2)** *(330 Bowery, Bond/Great Jones Sts.,)* is a handsome cast-iron building in a robust French Baroque style. Multiple banks, a fabric storage facility, and the Bouwerie Lane Theater (home to the Jean Cocteau Repertory Company) have occupied the space; currently, it is undergoing restoration, but is well worth a look. One of the finest of all New York's fire stations is the Beaux Arts **Fire Engine Company No. 33 (3)** *(44 Great Jones St., Lafayette St./ Bowery)*. And in a different style altogether, go see the vast Romanesque bulk of the **DeVinne Press Building (4)** *(393-399 Lafayette St. at E. Fourth St.)*, which once housed famous publications such as *Scribner's Monthly* and *Century Illustrated Monthly Magazine*.

Arts & Entertainment:

The **Merchant's House Museum (5)** *(29 E. Fourth St., Lafayette St./Bowery, 212-777-1089, www.merchants house.com; hours: M, Th–Su 12PM–5PM)* is like a little trip back to the 19th century. This delightful Federal house is decorated with the original furniture of the wealthy family that lived there for several generations, and offers exhibitions and tours that reveal early 19th-century domestic life. Another remnant of the elegant lives of this period's successful citizens can be found in the four remaining town houses of what was once called **Colonnade Row (6)** *(428-434 Lafayette St., Astor Pl./Great Jones St.)*. Check out the plays at the **Public Theater (7)** *(425 Lafayette St., Astor Pl./E. Fourth St., 212-539-8500, www. publictheater.org)*. If you're into the gallery scene, check out **Zürcher Studio (8)** *(33 Bleecker St., at Mott St., 212-777-0790, www. galeriezurcher.com; hours: Tu–Sa 12PM–6PM, Su 2PM–6PM)* for

painting, photography, video, sculpture, and installations by emerging artists from France and abroad.

PLACES TO EAT & DRINK
Where to Eat:

For great pizza at a great price, **A Slice of Naples (9) ($)** (*334B Bowery, Bond/Great Jones Sts., 212-466-3301, www.asliceofnaples.com; hours: Su–W 11AM–12AM, Th–Sa 11AM–4AM*) is perfect for a quick slice. The **Noho Star (10) ($$)** (*330 Lafayette St. at Bleecker St., 212-925-0070, www.nohostar.com; hours: M–F 7:30AM–11:30AM, Sa 10:30AM–12AM, Su 10:30AM–11PM*) dishes up good burgers and other American food, and the lively **Great Jones Café (11) ($$)** (*54 Great Jones St., Bowery/Lafayette Sts., 212-674-9304, www.greatjones.com; hours: Tu–F 12PM–4PM, M–Th 5PM–12AM, F–Sa 5PM–1AM, weekend brunch 11AM–4PM*) has tasty Southern cuisine. Top local Chef Marc Meyer's **Vic's (12) ($$)** (*31 Great Jones St., Bowery/Lafayette St., 212-253-5700, www.vicsnewyork.com; hours: M–F 12PM–11PM, Sa 5:30PM–11PM, Su 5:30PM–10PM, brunch Sa–Su 10:30AM–3PM*) features creative Italian-Mediterranean cuisine, and **BONDST (13) ($$$)** (*6 Bond St., Broadway/Lafayette St., 212-777-2500, www.bondst restaurant.com; hours: Su–Tu 6PM–10:30PM, W–Th 6PM–11PM, F–Sa 6PM–11:30PM*) is known for its sushi.

Bars & Nightlife:

Bar 288, also known as **Tom and Jerry's (14)** *(288 Elizabeth St., Bleecker/Houston Sts., 212-260-5045; hours: daily 12PM–4AM)*, has a wide selection of beers. For one of the neighborhood's best outdoor spaces, go to the former gas station now known as **B Bar and Grill (15)** *(40 E. Fourth St., Bowery/Lafayette St., 212-475-2220, www.bbarandgrill.com; hours: M 11AM–1AM, Tu–Th 11AM–2AM, F 11AM–4AM, Sa 10AM–4AM, Su 10AM–1AM)*. **Joe's Pub (16)** *(425 Lafayette St., Astor Place/E. Fourth St., 212-539-8500, www.joespub.com; hours: daily 6PM–1AM)*, located in the **Public Theater (7)**, is one of the most innovative and popular cabaret spots in the city.

WHERE TO SHOP

Along with art supplies, **Blick Art Materials (17)** *(1-5 Bond St., Broadway/Lafayette St., 212-533-2444, www.dickblick.com; hours: M–F 9AM–8PM, Sa 9AM–7PM, Su 11AM–6PM)* sells journals, stationery, and art books. If you're in the market for unique souvenirs, **Bond No. 9 New York (18)** *(9 Bond St., Broadway/Lafayette St., 212-228-1732, www.bondno9.com; hours: M–F 11AM–8PM, Sa 10AM–7PM, Su 12PM–6PM)* sells elegant perfumes named after different New York City locations. For CDs and DVDs, head to **Other Music (19)** *(15 E. 4th St., Broadway/Lafayette, 212-477-8150, www.othermusic.com; hours: M–F 11AM–9PM, Sa 12PM–8PM, Su 12PM–7PM)*, an indie-music mecca, which carries artists not found elsewhere and hosts in-store performances.

SOHO

● SNAPSHOT ●

The neighborhood now known as Soho has gone through many lives. In the years after the Civil War, its distinctive cast-iron warehouses housed many textile companies and other light manufacturers. By the mid-20th century, however, many of the manufacturers had moved on. Drawn by Soho's cobblestone streets, cheap rents, and huge loft spaces, many artists then made the neighborhood their own. In 1972, Soho was rezoned as a residential neighborhood as well as a manufacturing one, and the next year it was designated the SoHo Cast Iron Historic District. Rents began to soar. Today, it is the rare artist who can afford a Soho loft. The once half-empty streets of Soho are now packed with locals and tourists who come for the upscale trendy shopping and the galleries and museums.

PLACES TO SEE
Landmarks:

In the 19th century, cast iron was a popular building material. Strong and easily molded, a cast-iron facade could add elegance and durability to a plain brick build-ing. Soho has the largest collection of cast-iron buildings in the world. Both solid-looking and fanciful, these early precursors to the skyscraper give Soho a cinematic ambience. Some of the more famous buildings are the

Singer Building (20) *(561-563 Broadway, Prince/Spring Sts.)* and the E. V. Haughwout & Co. Store (21) *(488-492 Broadway, Spring/Broome Sts.).*

Arts & Entertainment:

The Angelika Film Center (22) *(18 W. Houston St. at Mercer St., 212-995-2570, www.angelikafilm center.com)* shows independent and art films. Come early to enjoy refreshments beneath a huge chandelier at the theater café. The Drawing Center (23) *(35 Wooster St., Broome/Grand Sts., 212-219-2166, www.drawingcenter.org; hours: W, F–Su 12PM–6PM, Th 12PM–8PM)* is a nonprofit gallery dedicated to promoting the art and appreciation of drawing. Artists Space (24) *(38 Greene St., Broome/Grand Sts., 3rd fl., 212-226-3970, www.artistsspace.org; hours: W–Su 12PM–6PM during exhibitions only)* is another nonprofit gallery that gives group shows focused on a theme. Many artists have gotten their start here. Among private galleries, Arcadia Fine Arts (25) *(51 Greene St., Broome/Grand Sts., 212-965-1387, www.arcadiafinearts.com; hours: M–F 10AM–6PM, Sa–Su 11AM–6PM)* and Janet Borden Gallery (26) *(560 Broadway, Prince/Spring Sts., 212-431-0166, www.janetbordeninc.com; hours: Tu–Sa 11AM–5PM)* are some of the most interesting. Animazing Gallery (27) *(54 Greene St., at Broome St., 212-226-7374, www. animazing.com; hours: M–Sa 10AM–7PM, Su 11AM–6PM)* includes illustration art by Maurice Sendak, Tim Burton, and other notable artists.

Kids:

The **New York City Fire Museum (28)** *(278 Spring St., Hudson/Varick Sts., 212-691-1303, www.nycfiremuseum. org; hours: daily 10AM–5PM)* is a 1904 firehouse that has a collection of old fire engines and equipment as well as displays dedicated to the history of firefighting, including the sad, heroic time during and after September 11, 2001.

PLACES TO EAT & DRINK
Where to Eat:

Pepe Rosso To Go (29) ($) *(149 Sullivan St., W. Houston/Prince Sts., 212-677-4555, www.peperossotogo. com; hours: daily 11AM–11PM)* started as an Italian takeout joint, but has added a few tables. Good pasta, great prices. When Soho was still a nameless artists' and factory neighborhood, **Fanelli's Cafe (30) ($$)** *(94 Prince St. at Mercer St., 212-226-9412; hours: daily 10AM– 2AM)*, a 19th-century bar, was practically the only watering hole. The restaurant is still a local favorite. Come for a beer, good food, and a glimpse of what things used to be like not so long ago. If you like tapas, try **Boqueria (31) ($-$$)** *(171 Spring St., 212-343-4255, www.boquerianyc.com; hours: Su–Th 12PM–10:30PM, F–Sa 12PM–11:30PM)*. This Soho spot reels in seafood lovers who enjoy small-plate dining. **Balthazar (32) ($$$)** *(80 Spring St., Broadway/Crosby St., 212-965- 1414, www.balthazarny.com; hours: continental break- fast M–F 7:30AM–11:30AM, Sa–Su 8AM–9AM; brunch Sa–Su 9AM–4PM; lunch M–F 12PM–5PM; dinner M– Th 6PM–12AM, F–Sa 6PM–1AM, Su 5:30PM–12AM)* is famous for its delicious French bistro food, turn-of-the-century French decor, and glamorous patrons. **Blue Ribbon Sushi (33) ($$)** *(97 Sullivan St., Prince/Spring Sts., 212-274-0404, www.blueribbon restaurants.com: daily 4PM–4AM)* is always crowded, and worth the wait. The restaurant is part of the small but excellent Blue Ribbon empire.

Bars & Nightlife:

What would an artists' neighborhood be without an old, dark, dive bar or two? Soho has a fair number. Besides **Fanelli's Cafe (30)** *(see page 76)*, there's the **Ear Inn (34)** *(326 Spring St., Greenwich/Washington Sts., 212-226-9060, www.earinn.com; hours: daily 12PM–4AM)*, which claims to be New York City's oldest bar, and the **Toad Hall (35)** *(57 Grand St., W. Broadway/Wooster St., 212-431-8145; hours: daily 12PM–4AM)*. For a quiet, casual evening, locals like **Emmett's (36)** *(50 Macdougal St., Houston/ Prince Sts., 212-639-3571, www.emmettsmacdougalst. com; hours: Tu 5:30PM–11PM, W–Sa 5:30PM–12AM, Sa 12PM–12AM, Su 12PM–11PM)* for its beer and Chicago-style deep-dish pizzas. **Pegu Club (37)** *(77 W. Houston St., 2nd Floor, West Broadway/Wooster Sts., 212-473-7348, www.peguclub.com, hours: Su–W 5PM–2AM, Th– Sa 5PM–4AM)* is a paradise for cocktail connoisseurs, by a luminary among bartenders. **City Winery (38)** *(155 Varick St. at Vandam, 212-608-0555; www.city winery.com; hours: M–F lunch 11:30AM–3PM, dinner Su–M 5PM–10PM, Tu–Sa 5PM–11PM)* serves their own wines and an impressive lineup of concerts.

Performing Garage (39) *(33 Wooster St., Broome/Grand Sts., 212-966-9796, www.thewoostergroup.org)*, an alternative theater, continues to be the home for a variety of innovative work. For music, the lineup at **Ear Inn (34)** is impressive. Listen to a variety of DJ-spun tunes at **The Anchor (40)** *(310 Spring St., Greenwich/Hudson Sts., 212-463-7406, www.theanchornyc.com; hours: Th–Sa 10PM–4AM)*. Dance the mambo or the merengue at **S.O.B.'s (41)** (Sounds of Brazil) *(204 Varick St., W. Houston/King Sts., 212-243-4940, www.sobs.com; call or look online for showtimes)*. This venerable club features live music not only from Brazil, but from all over Latin America, the Mideast, Africa, and the Caribbean.

WHERE TO SHOP

If you're in the market for ultra-chic, artsy clothing, and money is burning a hole in your pocket, Soho is the place. Anna Sui (42) *(113 Greene St., Prince/Spring Sts., 212-941-8406, www.annasui.com; hours: M–Sa 11:30AM–7PM, Su 12PM–6PM)*, Marc Jacobs (43) *(163 Mercer St., Houston/Prince Sts., 212-343-1490, www.marcjacobs.com; hours: M–Sa 11AM–7PM, Su 12PM–6PM)*, Anthropologie (44) *(375 West Broadway, Spring/Broome Sts., 212-343-7070, www.anthropologie.com; hours: M–Sa 10AM–9PM, Su 10AM–8PM)*, and Prada (45) *(575 Broadway at Prince St., 212-334-8888, www.prada.com; hours: M–Sa 11AM–8PM, Su 12PM–7PM)* are just a few destinations. Add cooler-than-thou European shoes from Camper (46) *(125 Prince St. at Wooster St., 212-358-1842, www.camper.com; hours: M–Sa 11AM–8PM, Su 12PM–6PM)*. Or try Kenneth Cole New York (47) *(595 Broadway, Houston/Prince Sts., 212-965-0283, www.kennethcole.com; hours: M–W 10AM–8PM,*

Th–Sa 10AM–9PM, *Su* 11AM–7PM). For colorful statement jewelry, watches, handbags, and accessories, Folli Follie (48) (*133 Prince St., 212-780-5555, www.follifollie.com; hours: M–Sa* 11AM–7PM, *Su* 12PM–6PM) offers plenty of artfully-designed items worth toting home. For a fun, hidden underneath-gift for yourself or your partner, some sexy lingerie from Agent Provocateur (49) (*133 Mercer St., Prince/Spring Sts., 212-965-0229, www.agentprovocateur. com; hours: M–Sa* 11AM–7PM, *Su* 12PM–6PM) is a perfect choice. Sadly, the Chinatown institution Pearl River Mart (50) is closing in December. (*477 Broadway, Broome/ Grand Sts., 212-431-4770, www.pearlriver.com; hours: daily* 10AM–7:20PM). Check their website to see if they have relocated and to buy gorgeous silk jackets, blouses, porcelain, teas, lighting, and souvenirs at bargain prices. And the collection of exquisite journals, stationery, and handmade papers at Kate's Paperie (51) (*188 Lafayette, Broome/Grand Sts., 212-941-9816, www.katespaperie. com; hours: M–W* 10AM–7PM, *Th–Sa* 10AM–8PM, *Su* 11:30AM–7PM) will make you want to write home.

WHERE TO STAY

The Mercer (52) ($$$$) (*188 Lafayette, Broome/Grand Sts., 212-966-6060, www.mercerhotel.com*) has high-fashion interiors, marble bathrooms, a 24-hour concierge and room service, in a heart-of-Soho locale. The Holiday Inn Downtown/Soho (53) ($$-$$$) (*138 Lafayette St., Canal/Howard Sts., 212-966-8898, www.holidayinn. com*) is pleasant, clean, convenient, and cheap (for the neighborhood).

Ⓐ Ⓒ Ⓔ *to West Fourth St. or 14th St.;*
Ⓑ Ⓓ Ⓕ Ⓜ *to West Fourth St.;* Ⓕ Ⓜ *to 14th St.;*
❶ ❷ ❸ *to 14th St.;* ❶ *to Christopher St.*

● SNAPSHOT ●

"The Village" has long been a refuge and one of the city's most-coveted neighborhoods. In the 17th and 18th centuries, it was a sleepy country town to which New Yorkers fled in order to escape various plagues. In the 19th century, Italian immigrants arrived, bringing their cafés, bakeries, churches, and pizzerias with them. These days, the crooked tree-lined streets of the Village are prime celebrity-spotting territory, as many actors and models have made it their home. But more than anything, this neighborhood has always drawn those attracted by its air of tolerance. The list of writers, painters, actors, musicians, and revolutionaries who have lived or hung out in this neighborhood would fill an encyclopedia. Among them are Edgar Allan Poe, Mark Twain, Edna St. Vincent Millay, Richard Wright, Jack Kerouac, Edward Hopper, Cary Grant,

John Barrymore, Bob Dylan, and John Reed, and that's just for starters. The Village is also where many say the gay liberation movement was born— on June 28, 1969, to be exact, when a police raid on The Stonewall Inn, a gay bar at 51 Christopher Street, evolved into the Stonewall Riots. The

Stonewall Inn has moved to 53 Christopher Street, and the surrounding neighborhood, with its bars and clubs, is still considered a gay center.

PLACES TO SEE
Landmarks:

There are two things to realize before you begin your tour of the Village. First, the Village was not built on a numbered grid system, the way most of Manhattan was, but grew organically out of a network of rural paths. The result is some crazy cartographical anomalies, such as the corner where West 12th Street crosses West Fourth. It's easy to get lost, and even locals rely on their smartphone maps from time to time. When you turn down some surprising alleyway, you'll soon discover that getting lost is part of the fun. The other thing to keep in mind is that there are really two villages: Greenwich Village, whose central plaza is Washington Square Park, and the West Village, the area surrounding Sheridan Square.

A good place to start a Greenwich Village tour is at **Washington Square Park (54)**, at the base of Fifth Avenue. Once a potter's field and a site for public hangings, this park is a haven for guitar strummers, chess players, street performers, NYU students, and those reliving the area's beatnik past. Its most notable feature is the **Washington Square Arch** *(NE side of Washington Square)*, designed by the architect Stanford White and erected in 1895 to commemorate George Washington's

inauguration. Check out the elegant Greek revival town houses on **Washington Square North**. When they were built in the 1830s, they were some of the most exclusive residences in town. Henry James's grandmother owned one. Now most of them are owned by **NYU**. Its campus is scattered in buildings all over Greenwich Village. You might also want to peek in at **Washington Mews (55)** *(Washington Square North and East Eighth St.)*. This quaint cobblestone street was once where the horses of the aristocracy were stabled and the servants lived. The **Brown Building (56)** *(23-29 Washington Place, at Greene St.)*, now home to classrooms and offices of **NYU**, was previously the **Triangle Shirtwaist Factory Building**—the site of a tragic fire in 1911 which claimed the lives of 146 workers, most of them young women. Two years earlier it had been the site of one of the first major strikes by women workers in the history of the United States. One of the union's major complaints was the need for fire safety. Those needs were ignored and two years later missing fire escapes and locked doors were to blame for one of the worst industrial disasters in America. The fire led to major labor reform. Although the building is closed to the public, there is a plaque commemorating the workers at the corner of the building.

The streets around Washington Square were popular in the 1950s, 1960s, and early 1970s with abstract expressionists, folkies, beatniks, and war resisters. Washington Square South turns into **West Fourth Street (57)**, the inspiration for Bob Dylan's "Positively Fourth Street." Sullivan, Thompson, Bleecker, and MacDougal streets were once places to catch a wild poetry reading, buy some handmade sandals or silver jewelry, and sip a cappuccino in the days long before there was a Starbucks on every corner. The handmade sandals, and the beatniks who wore them, are gone, but plenty of cafés remain, still pleasant places to while away an afternoon. Try **Caffé Reggio (58)** *(119 MacDougal St. at W. Third St., 212-475-9557, www.caffereggio.com; hours: M–Th 8AM–3AM, F–Sa 8AM–4:30AM, Su 9AM–3AM)*, **Joe (59)** *(141 Waverly Pl., Gay St./6th Ave., 212-924-6750, www.joenewyork. com; hours: M–F 7AM–8PM, Sa–Su 8AM–8PM)*, or **Caffe Dante (60)** *(79 MacDougal St., Bleecker/W. Houston Sts., 212-982-5275, www.caffedante.com; hours: Su–Th 10AM–1AM, F–Sa 10AM–2AM)*. For those interested in the history of rock, there's Jimi Hendrix's **Electric Lady Sound Studios (61)** *(52 W. Eighth St., Fifth/Sixth Aves., 212-677-4700, www.electricladystudios.com)*.

Along with the Washington Arch, Greenwich Village's most distinctive architectural landmark is the **Jefferson Market Library (62)** *(425 Sixth Ave., W. 9th/W. 10th Sts., 212-243-4334; hours: M, W 10AM–8PM; Tu, Th 11AM–6PM; F–Sa 10AM–5PM)*. This red brick castle with its fairy-tale watchtower was originally designed as a courthouse by the Central Park designer Calvert Vaux in 1876. Vacated in 1945, it stood empty for 20 years and was slated for demolition when the efforts of community organizers resulted in the current renovation. It was opened as a public library in 1967. There are some charming streets in this area. Among them are **Patchin Place (63)** *(off W. 10th St., Greenwich/Sixth*

Aves.), a quiet iron-gated mews containing a number of three-story houses (4 Patchin Place was the home of poet e. e. cummings). **West 11th Street** *(Fifth/Sixth Aves.)* and **West 12th Street** *(Fifth/Sixth Aves.)* is where **The New School (64)** *(66 West 12th St., www.newschool.edu)*—founded by radical intellectuals in 1919—is located.

A walk west will take you toward Greenwich Village's other square, **Sheridan Square (65)** *(Commerce St./W. Fourth St./Seventh Ave.),* though in true got-to-be-different Village style, it's actually more of a triangle. Nearby Bedford Street is known for two houses that stand next to each other: **77 Bedford (66)** *(Morton/Commerce Sts.)*—the Isaac-Hendricks House—the oldest house in the Village, built in 1799; and **75-1/2 Bedford (66)**, only nine-and-a-half-feet wide, once the home of Edna St. Vincent Millay and later John Barrymore. The **Church of St. Luke's in the Fields (67)** *(487 Hudson St., Grove/Christopher Sts., 212-924-0562, www.stlukeinthe fields.org; hours: open for prayer and meditation M–F 10AM–2PM, 5:45PM–7PM, Su 7:30AM–3PM or until 1PM in summer),* built in 1822, is one of the lovelier churches in the city. And if you're getting tired of quaint, amble over to the glass towers of **Perry West (68)** *(176 Perry St., corner of West St.).* This apartment complex, designed by the modernist architect Richard Meier and opened in 2003, is home to several celebrities.

Opened in Spring 2015, the **Whitney Museum of American Art (69)** *(99 Gansevoort St. at Washington St., 212-570-3600, www.whitney.org; hours: M, W, Su 10:30AM–6PM, Th, F, Sa 10:30AM–10PM, closed Tu)* brings its collection, housed in a dramatically modern building designed by architect Renzo Piano, to the **Meatpacking District**. This area is best seen at night, when the combination of old warehouses, old memories, and up-to-the-minute bistros, bars, and clubs creates a very urban glamour.

Arts & Entertainment:

The famous poet and Greenwich Village resident Edna St. Vincent Millay was the founder of the **Cherry Lane Theatre (70)** *(38 Commerce St., Seventh Ave./Bedford St., 212-989-2020, www.cherrylanetheatre.org)*. Begun in 1924, it was the first off-Broadway theater, and still hosts experimental theater, mixing it with more mainstream productions. Its tiny space offers an intimate theatrical experience. **Barrow Street Theatre (71)** *(27 Barrow Street, at Seventh Ave., 212-868-4444, www.barrowstreet theatre.com)* is another off-Broadway spot that garners widespread attention. If you like stand-up, the **Comedy Cellar (72)** *(117 MacDougal St., W. Third/Bleecker Sts., 212-254-3480, www.comedy cellar.com; Check website or call for showtimes)* is one of the more prestigious places for comics, and big names such as Jerry Seinfeld and Ray Romano make frequent appearances to brush up on their audience skills. The Village, for all its attractions, isn't a museum hot spot, but it is the site of one of the best, and certainly the quirkiest, small museums in New York, the **Forbes Magazine Galleries (74)** *(62 Fifth Ave. at W. 12th St., 212-206-5548, www.forbesgalleries.com, entrance is free;*

hours: Tu–Sa 10AM–4PM). The late gazillionaire Malcolm Forbes was a man who liked to have fun, and the gallery is a memorial to his passions, from toy boats to stray pieces of memorabilia, all arranged with wit and a touchingly personal sense. NYU offers its own exhibition space with the little-known but absolutely first-rate **Grey Art Gallery (75)** *(NYU Silver Center, 100 Washington Square East, corner of Washington Pl., 212-998-6780, www.nyu. edu/greyart; hours: Tu, Th, F 11AM–6PM, W 11AM–8PM, Sa 11AM–5PM),* featuring a 6,000-piece permanent collection of late 19th-century to early 20th-century art, including works by Picasso, de Kooning, and Miró.

Kids:

It may scare younger or more sensitive kids, but the annual **Halloween Day Parade** *(www.halloween-nyc.com)* that snakes its way up Sixth Avenue every October is incredible fun. A mix of ghosts, goblins, superheroes, stilt-walkers, drag queens, and, inevitably, endless Elvis Presleys, all wow the good-natured crowd. The **Carmine Street Playground**  (76) *(32 Carmine St., Bleecker/Bedford Sts.)* is one of the best in the Village. Head through the narrow passageway into a delightful safe play area full of climbing frames and toys.

PLACES TO EAT & DRINK
Where to Eat:

Although the Village certainly has some expensive (and worth it) restaurants, a budget traveler can eat extremely well here. In fact, some of the Village's most popular restaurants are also among its most reasonable. For breakfast-to-go, grab baked goods from **Magnolia Bakery (77) ($)** *(401 Bleecker St. at W. 11th St., 212-462-2572, www.magnoliabakery.com; hours: Su–Th 9AM–11:30PM, F–Sa 9AM–12:30AM).* The creative sandwiches served at **Peanut Butter & Co. (78) ($)** *(240 Sullivan St. at W. 3rd St., 212-677-3995, www.ilovepeanutbutter.com; hours: Su–Th 11AM–9PM, F–Sa 11AM–10PM)* makes it clear that peanut butter isn't just for lunchboxes anymore. For New York pizza, **John's of Bleecker Street Pizzeria (79) ($)** *(278 Bleecker St., Sixth/Seventh Aves., 212-243-1680, www.johnsbrickovenpizza.com; hours: M–Th 11:30AM–*

11:30PM, F 11:30AM–12AM, Sa 11:30AM–12:30AM, Su 12PM–11:30PM) has been serving customers brick-oven

pies since the 1920s. (The only caveat: John's does not serve slices, so bring a big appetite or a group to share a pie.) For inexpensive Middle Eastern fare, try **Moustache (80) ($)** *(90 Bedford St., Barrow/ Grove Sts., 212-229-2220, www. moustachepitza.com; hours: daily 12PM–12AM).* On a rainy afternoon you might enjoy high tea at **Tea & Sympathy (81) ($$)** *(108 Greenwich Ave., W. 12th/W. 13th Sts., 212-989-9735, www.teaandsympathynewyork.com; hours: M–F 11:30AM–10:30PM, Sa–Su 9:30AM–10:30PM),* served in an eccentric English atmosphere. If you're in the mood for a blow out, try **Pastis (82) ($$)** *(9 Ninth Ave. at Little 12th St., 212-929-4844, www.pastisny.com; hours: breakfast M–F 8AM–11:30AM, lunch M–F 12PM–6PM, brunch Sa–Su 9AM–4:30PM, dinner daily 6PM–12AM, supper Su–W 12PM–1AM, Th 12PM–2AM, F–Sa 12PM–3AM),* a raucous French bistro in the Meatpacking District, for oysters and a glimpse at the beautiful people. Italian food is always a good choice in the Village. **Babbo (83) ($$$)** *(110 Waverly Pl., MacDougal St./Sixth Ave.,*

212-777-0303, www.babbonyc.com; hours: Tu–Sa 11:30AM–1:30PM, M–Sa 5:30PM–11:30PM, Su 5PM–11PM; wine bar open M–Sa 5PM, Su 4:30PM), owned by superstar chef and local character, Mario Batali, remains a local favorite. Or, try some authentic Peruvian cuisine—and a pisco sour—at **Panca (84) ($$)** (*92 Seventh Ave South. near Barrow St., 212-488-3900; www.pancany.com; hours: M–W 12PM–10PM, Th 12PM–11PM, F–Su 12PM–12AM*). Finally, if all this cosmopolitanism gives you a craving for good American food and moderate prices, **Jane (85) ($$)** (*100 W. Houston St., La Guardia Pl./Thompson St., 212-254-7000, www.janerestaurant. com; hours: M–Th 11:30AM–11PM, F 11:30AM–12AM, Sa 11AM–12AM, Su 10AM–10PM*) serves chops, seafood, and deliciously gooey desserts in an understated elegant setting.

Bars & Nightlife:

White Horse Tavern (86) (*567 Hudson St. at W. 11th St., 212-989-3956; hours: Su–Th 11AM–2AM, F–Sa 11AM–4AM*), is where poet Dylan Thomas went on his last drinking binge before dying a few hours later. The former biker bar, **Hogs and Heifers (87)** (*859 Washington St. at W. 13th St., 212-929-0655, www.hogsand heifers.com; hours: M–F 11AM–4AM, Sa 1PM–4AM, Su 2PM–4AM*) is not nearly as down-and-dirty as it once was, though the walls are still decorated with discarded bras. For one of the neighborhood's best beer lists—and bar food made from locally-sourced ingredients—squeeze into **Wilfie & Nell (88)** (*228 W. Fourth St., Seventh Ave./W. 10th St., 212-242-2990; www.wilfie andnell.com; hours: M–W 4PM–3AM, Th–F 4PM–4AM, Sa–Su 12PM–4AM*). Craving a good glass of red? Head to **8th Street Winecellar (89)** (*28 W. Eighth St. near*

Fifth Ave., 212-260-9463; www.8thstwinecellar.com; hours: daily 4PM–2AM). The **Monster (90)** *(80 Grove St., Waverly Pl./W. Fourth St., 212-924-3558, www. manhattan-monster.com; hours: M–F 4PM–4AM, Sa– Su 2PM–4AM)* is one of the area's most popular

gay hangouts. The Village is the home of some famous jazz clubs, such as the **Village Vanguard (91)** *(178 Seventh Ave. South, corner of W. 11th St., 212-255-4037, www.village vanguard.com; hours: sets at 8:30PM and 10:30PM nightly, doors open at 7:30PM)* and the **Blue Note (92)** *(131 W. Third St., MacDougal St./Sixth Ave., 212-475-8592, www. bluenotejazz.com; hours: shows Su–F at 8PM and 10:30PM, additional shows F, Sa 12:30AM).* These famous clubs can be pricey, however. Some inexpensive (and very popular) clubs to try are the **55 Bar (93)** *(55 Christopher St., Sixth/Seventh Aves., 212-929-9883, www.55bar.com; daily music)* and **The Bitter End (94)** *(147 Bleecker St., Thompson St./La Guardia Pl., 212-673-7030, www.bitterend.com; check schedule for daily music)*, where legends like Bob Dylan and Billy Joel have played. **Zinc Bar (95)** *(82 W. 3rd St., Thompson/Sullivan Sts., 212-477-9462 www.zincbar. com; hours: Su–Th 6PM–2:30AM, F–Sa 6PM–3AM)* has a variety of sounds featured, including Brazilian jazz, jazz vocals, and poetry readings.

WHERE TO SHOP

One of the first fashion designers to head to the Meatpacking District was Jeffrey New York (96) *(449 W. 14th St., Ninth/10th Aves., 212-206-1272, www. jeffreynewyork.com; hours: M–W, F 10AM–8PM, Th 10AM–9PM, Sa 10AM–7PM, Su 12:30PM–6PM)*, which sells spendy but beautiful clothing and shoes. Somewhat more downmarket is Urban Outfitters (97) *(374 Sixth Ave. at Waverly Pl., 212-677-9350, www.urbanoutfit ters.com; hours: M–W 10AM–9PM, Th–Sa 10AM–10PM, Su 10AM–8PM)*, which sells hipster gear and housewares for those on a budget.  For something sexy to wear beneath, La Petite Coquette (98) *(51 University Pl., W. Ninth/W. 10th Sts., 212-473-2478, www. thelittleflirt.com; hours: M–Sa 11AM–7PM, Su 12PM–6PM)* is a good choice for gorgeous lingerie. New Yorkers looking for cheap fashionable shoes will browse the shoe stores on West 8th Street (99) *(Fifth/Sixth Aves.)*.

C. O. Bigelow (100) has been standing at 414 Sixth Avenue *(W. Eighth/W. Ninth Sts., 212-533-2700, www.bigelow chemists.com; hours: M–F 7:30AM–9PM, Sa 8:30AM–7PM, Su 8:30AM–5:30PM)* for more than 150 years. It offers a quirky collection of American and European lotions and soaps. The streets around Bleecker and Sixth Avenue have many shops catering to the music lover. Vinyl enthusiasts should head straight to Rebel Rebel

Records (101) *(319 Bleecker St., Christopher/Grove Sts., 212-989-0770; hours: Su–W 12PM–8PM, Th–Sa 12PM–9PM)* or **Bleecker Street Records (102)** *(239 Bleecker St., Carmine/Leroy Sts., 212-255-7899, www.bleeckerstreetrecordsnyc.com; hours: Su–Th 11AM–10PM, F–Sa 11AM–11PM)*.

Matt Umanov Guitars (103) *(273 Bleecker St., Sixth/Seventh Aves., 212-675-2157, www.umanovguitars.com; hours: M–Sa 11AM–7PM, Su 12PM–6PM)* has long been famous for its collection of both acoustic and electric instruments. One of the city's best independent bookstores is **Three Lives & Company (104)** *(154 W. 10th St. at Waverly Pl., 212-741-2069, www.threelives.com; hours: Su 12PM–7PM, M–Tu 12PM–8PM, W–Sa 11AM–8:30PM)*, which has a knowledgeable staff and an excellent selection of literary fiction, biography, and memoirs. Shopping for food in the Village is an experience that is miles away from pushing your cart through the supermarket. Foodies love the venerable **Murray's Cheese Shop (105)** *(254 Bleecker St., Sixth/Seventh Aves., 212-243-3289, www.murrayscheese.com; hours: M–Sa 8AM–9PM, Su 9AM–7PM)*, opened in 1940. For a pound or two of freshly roasted coffee, go to **Porto Rico Importing Co. (106)** *(201 Bleecker St., Sixth Ave./MacDougal St., 212-477-5421, www.portorico.com; hours: M–F 8AM–9PM, Sa 9AM–9PM, Su 12PM–7PM)*, a family-owned business that began in 1907. For a taste of high designer fashion, check out **Cynthia Rowley (107)** *(376 Bleecker St., Perry/Charles*

Sts., 212-242-3803, *www.cynthiarowley.com; hours: M–F 10AM–8PM, Sa–Su 11AM–8PM)* for women's clothing, handbags, eyewear, and shoes. If chess is your game, head to Thompson Street. **The Chess Forum (108)** *(219 Thompson St., W. Third/Bleecker Sts., 212-475-3905, www.chessforum.com, hours: daily 11AM–12AM)* sells beautiful chess sets and other chess-related paraphernalia.

WHERE TO STAY

It's expensive, but the **Hotel Gansevoort (110) ($$$$)** *(18 Ninth Ave. at W. 13th St., 212-206-6700, www.hotel gansevoort.com)* in the Meatpacking District is a stylish building with generous-sized rooms, a private roof garden, and a pool. The **Washington Square Hotel (111) ($$-$$$)** *(103 Waverly Place, MacDougal St./Sixth Ave., 212-777-9515, www.wshotel.com)* is a comfortable 100-year-old building in a great location across from the square. Rooms aren't big, but it's reasonably priced and friendly. The **Larchmont Hotel (112) ($-$$)** *(27 W. 11th St., Fifth/Sixth Aves., 212-989-9333, www. larchmonthotel.com)* is great if you don't mind sharing a bathroom. This small hotel on a beautiful Greenwich Village street has tons of European-style charm: clean, nicely furnished rooms with ceiling fans, and a complimentary continental breakfast. An elegant town house located in Greenwich Village, the **West Eleventh Bed and Breakfast (113) ($$-$$$)** *(278 West 11th St., Bleecker/W. 4th Sts., 212-675-7897, www.west-eleventh.com)*, is known for its handsomely furnished rooms and homey atmosphere.

UNION SQUARE

L N Q R 4 5 6 *to 14th St.-Union Square*

● SNAPSHOT ●

Union Square is the city's most historic gathering place. It has been the scene of innumerable labor rallies and war protests and, in the days after September 11, 2001, it was the site of an impromptu shrine. Most people come to Union Square these days either to sell produce or to buy it; the city's busiest farmers' market is based here. Union Square is also home to restaurants, stores, and ultra-hip hotels.

PLACES TO SEE
Landmarks:

On Tuesdays, Thursdays, and Sundays, Union Square is a busy transportation hub, a place to walk the dog and gape at the statues of George Washington, Lafayette, and Gandhi. On Mondays, Wednesdays, Fridays, and Saturdays, farmers, bakers, a hard pretzel vendor, and more set up shop. Even if you're not up for food shopping, the **Union Square Greenmarket (114)** *(N. end, Broadway/Park Ave. S.)* is a good place to spot celebrity chefs, and celebrities shopping for flowers or fruit. In the 1960s, **33 Union Square West (115)** *(near corner of E. 16th St.)* was the home of something far less bucolic: Andy Warhol's Factory. Those interested in New York history

95

might want to take a look at the **Union Square Theatre (116)** *(100 E. 17th St., at Union Square East, www.newyork citytheatre.com/theaters/unionsquaretheatre/theatre.php)*. In the 19th century, it was the headquarters of the infamous Tammany Hall, the corrupt political machine that, led by William Tweed, robbed the city coffers, but started building both Central Park and the Brooklyn Bridge, so perhaps it was a fair exchange.

Arts & Entertainment:

The major draw for most people here is the incredible **Greenmarket (114)** *(see page 95)*, but if you're a theater fan, you're in luck: the area has two of the hippest and most fun theaters, the **Union Square Theatre (116)** and the **Daryl Roth Theatre (117)** *(101 E. 15th St. at Union Square East, 212-375-1110, www.darylroth theatre.com)*. Both seem to specialize in putting on experimental and "out-of-the-box" shows (the infamous *De La Guarda*, which ran at the Daryl Roth, for example), full of messy audience participation that kids and teenagers love, though they may well leave theater-goers with more traditional tastes cold. The **Vineyard Theatre (118)** *(108 E. 15th St., 4th Ave./Irving Pl., 212-353-0303, www.vine yardtheatre.org)* also offers adventurous choices; *Avenue Q*, the Tony Award-winning musical, got its start here.

Kids:

Union Square has two playgrounds, enclosed and with safety rubber matting, though they can get pretty crowded. Local skateboarders roll and jump through the northern end of the square when the Greenmarket is not in operation, which is safely cordoned off from traffic.

PLACES TO EAT & DRINK
Where to Eat:

For good comfort food with a Brazilian twist and excellent people-watching, check out **Coffee Shop (119) ($$)** (*29 Union Square West, 212-243-7969, www.thecoffee shopnyc.com, hours: M 7AM–2AM, Tu 7AM–4AM, W–F 7AM–5:30AM, Sa 8AM–5:30AM, Su 8AM–2AM*). **15 East (120) ($$$$)** (*15 E. 15th St., Fifth Ave./Union Sq. W, 212-647-0015, www.15eastrestaurant.com; hours: M–F 12PM–1:30PM, 6PM–10:30PM, Sa 6PM–11PM*) will satisfy your Japanese cravings—for a pretty penny, but it's worth it. For great Middle Eastern sandwiches, **Rainbow Falafel and Shawarma (121) ($)** (*26 E. 17th St., Fifth Ave./Broadway, 212-691-8641, takeout only; hours: M–Sa 11AM–7PM*) is the place. Union Square also has several chic (albeit pricey) restaurants. The one that started it all is the **Union Square Café (122) ($$$)** (*21 E. 16th St., Fifth Ave./Union Square West, 212-243-4020, www.unionsquarecafe.com; hours: M–Th 12PM–10PM, F 12PM–11PM, Sa 11AM–11PM, Su 11AM–10PM*). Its friendly service and creative American cuisine make it one of the most popular restaurants in New York. Some other good choices are the **Blue Water Grill (123) ($$$)** (*31 Union Square West at E. 16th St., 212-675-9500, www.bluewatergrillnyc. com; hours: Su 10:30AM–10PM, M 11:30AM–10PM, Tu–Th 11:30AM–11PM, F–Sa 11:30AM–12AM*) for seafood, and **ABC Kitchen (124) ($$$)** (*35 E. 18th St., Broadway/Park Ave. South, 212-475-5829, www.abc kitchennyc.com; hours: dinner M–W 5:30PM–10:30PM, Th 5:30PM–11PM, F–Sa 5:30PM–11:30PM, Su 5:30PM–10PM,*

lunch M–F 12PM–3PM, brunch Sa–Su 11AM–3:30PM), where superchef Jean-Georges Vongerichten serves up locally-sourced American Nouveau cuisine in a unique setting.

Bars & Nightlife:

If you're a fan of late night talk shows, the **Old Town Bar & Grill (125)** *(45 E. 18th St., Broadway/Park Ave. South, 212-529-6732, www.oldtownbar.com; hours: M–Sa 11:30AM–1AM, Su 1PM–12AM)* might look familiar: it's featured in the opening credits of *The Late Show with David Letterman.* This 19th-century tavern is a great place to grab a beer and good bar food. **Pete's Tavern (126)** *(129 E. 18th St. at Irving Pl., 212-473-7676, www.petestavern.com; hours: daily 11AM–2:30AM)* is another classic NY bar: supposedly O. Henry hung out here. The standing tables at the front of **Republic (127)** *(37 Union Square West, 16th/17th Sts., 212-627-7172; www.thinknoodles.com; hours: Su–W 11:30AM–10:30PM, Th–Sa 11:30AM–11:30PM)* offer an easy spot to perch with a drink and chat with locals

waiting to meet up with friends. And if you're looking for something exclusive and quietly hip, go to **The Living Room Lounge (128)** *(201 Park Ave. South at E. 17th St., 212-930-7444, starwoodhotels. com/whotels; hours: Su–W 11AM–2AM, Th–Sa 11AM–3AM)* inside the trendy **W New York-Union Square Hotel (131)**. **Irving Plaza (129)** *(17 Irving Pl., E. 15th/16 Sts.,*

212-777-6800, www.irvingplaza.com) is one of the best rock venues in town, host to medium-sized bands and the occasional big name playing a smaller show.

WHERE TO SHOP

For sporting goods, Paragon Sports (130) *(867 Broadway at E. 18th St., 212-255-8889, www.paragonsports.com; hours: M–F 10AM–8:30PM, Sa 10AM–8PM, Su 11AM–7PM)* is a local favorite.

WHERE TO STAY

If you don't mind forking out some serious dough, there's always the W New York-Union Square Hotel (131) ($$$$) *(201 Park Ave. South at E. 17th St., 212-253-9119, www.wnewyorkunionsquare.com).* It's housed in a fabulous old building just off Union Square, and has a handsome bar on the ground floor in which to watch the elegant clientele at play.

chapter 4

CHELSEA

GARMENT DISTRICT

TIMES SQUARE-THEATER DISTRICT

& HELL'S KITCHEN

CHELSEA
GARMENT DISTRICT
TIMES SQUARE-
THEATER DISTRICT
& HELL'S KITCHEN

Places to See:

1. Chelsea Hotel
2. 437-459 West 24th Street
3. Cushman Row
4. Starrett-Lehigh Building
5. High Line
6. London Terrace
7. Chelsea Piers
8. Hudson River Park
9. Agora Gallery
10. The Kitchen
11. Museum at the Fashion Institute of Technology
12. Gagosian Gallery
13. Rubin Museum of Art
14. Joyce Theater
39. Lesbian, Gay, Bisexual & Transgender Community Center
40. Gay Men's Health Crisis
44. Macy's
45. Herald Square
46. Greeley Square
47. Madison Square Garden
48. Penn Station
49. General Post Office
52. New York Times Building (original)
53. New York Times Building
54. NASDAQ MarketSite
55. Reuters Building
56. 4 Times Square
57. Brill Building
58. Music Row
59. Time & Life Building
60. Lyceum Theatre
61. Ed Sullivan Theater
62. Winter Garden Theater
63. Al Hirschfeld Theater
64. TKTS Booth
65. Times Square Visitors Center
66. Carnegie Hall/Zankel Hall
67. Town Hall
68. Madame Tussauds New York
69. Circle Line
70. Intrepid Sea-Air-Space Museum
71. On Location Tours

CHELSEA

A C E *to 14th Street;* **C E** *to 23rd Street;*
1 *to 18th St. or 23rd St.*

• SNAPSHOT •

Originally the country estate of a sea captain, Chelsea evolved into a sophisticated urban area with handsome Greek and Italian town houses, great swaths of which still survive and make it one of the most desirable residential areas in the city. Nowadays, Chelsea is primarily renowned for two things that other neighborhoods were once famous for: the gay scene, which has largely migrated from the Village; and the art scene, which became increasingly priced out of Soho. There's also Chelsea's waterfront, which in recent years has seen remarkable development, as have long stretches of the rest of the city's long-neglected waterfront.

PLACES TO SEE
Landmarks:

If it's your first visit to Chelsea, don't miss a visit to the legendary **Chelsea Hotel (1)** *(222 West 23rd St., Seventh/Eighth Aves., 646-918-7770, www.hotelchelsea.com).* This wonderful building with its beautiful rows of cast-iron balconies started life as one of the city's first co-ops, before becoming a hotel in 1905. Its famous clientele has included Tennessee Williams, Mark Twain, Bob Dylan, and Sid Vicious to name a few. Unfortunately, the hotel is closed for interior renovations; however, the dramatic exterior is still worth walking by. For architecture buffs, two blocks in particular are outstanding for their surviving period details: **437-459 West 24th Street (2)** *(Ninth/Tenth Aves.)*—a row of late Italianate brick houses—and the so-called **Cushman Row (3)** *(406-418 W. 20th St., Ninth/Tenth Aves.)*. On a more modern note, the **Starrett-Lehigh Building (4)** *(601 W. 26th St., Eleventh/ Twelfth Aves., www.starrett-lehigh.com)* is one of the city's gems. Designed as a warehouse in 1930–1931, complete with rail tracks leading directly into it, it now leads a less rugged life as home to a cluster of Web designers, media outlets, and the like. It's not a building, but one of Chelsea's most interesting landmarks is the **High Line (5)**, a long-defunct elevated rail track that runs above and just west of Tenth Avenue from around Gansevoort St. to 34th St., entering and exiting numerous industrial buildings and bumping up against several apartment buildings. It has turned into a park and is now an elevated green walkway. Confirming that everything New York is on a grand scale, **London Terrace (6)** *(W. 23rd/W. 24th Sts., Ninth/Tenth Aves., www.londonterracetowers.com)* is a vast apartment building with more than 4,000 rooms occupying an entire square block. Its original developer, who envisioned it as a bastion of British chic complete with doormen dressed as British Bobbies, went bankrupt in the 1930s, and threw him-self off the roof. You may see professional dog walkers and their noisy packs entering or exiting the building. Heading over to the river you'll encounter the popular

Chelsea Piers (7) *(Piers 59-62, W. 17th/W. 23rd Sts., Eleventh Avenue to the Hudson River, 212-336-6666, www.chelseapiers.com)*, which houses a vast sports complex where you can rock climb, bowl, in-line skate, roller-skate, shoot hoops, and even whack golf balls out toward the Hudson River and into a giant net. There are also a number of bars and restaurants, and fancy docking facilities for the private yachts that berth here. Many sailboat and other small-ship Hudson River cruises leave from the Chelsea Piers docks. On a warm day, benches on the waterfront provide a pleasant place to sit and relax. If Chelsea Piers isn't your thing, you can simply walk or blade away along the waterfront esplanade and park that forms the **Hudson River Park (8)** *(www.hudsonriverpark.org)*, which under various guises forms a border of green along most of the west side of Manhattan.

GAY CHELSEA

There are numerous publications that list gay and lesbian events around the city, many of which are free and available in street corner boxes. In particular, check out weeklies *Next* and *Gay City News*. Gay and lesbian visitors can count on the Lesbian, Gay, Bisexual & Transgender Community Center (39) *(208 W. 13th St., Seventh/Eighth Aves., 212-620-7310, www.gaycenter.org)*, located slightly south of Chelsea on 13th Street, for information on anything from health issues to simply what's happening around town. More specifically for HIV counseling and advice, there's the venerable Gay Men's Health Crisis (40) *(446 W. 33rd Street, 212-367-1000, www.gmhc.org)*. There are countless bars to suit every taste and mood. Barracuda (41) *(275 W. 22nd St., Seventh/Eighth Aves., 212-645-8613; hours: daily 4PM–4AM)* serves up everything from a quiet place to chat to bawdy drag queen shows. Gym Sportsbar (42) *(167 Eighth Ave., 18th/19th Sts., 212-337-2439; www.gymsportsbar.com; hours: M–Th 4PM–2AM, F 4PM–4AM, Sa 1PM–4AM, Su 1PM–2AM)* is the city's only gay sports bar. The Chelsea Mews Guest House (43) *(344 W. 15th St., Eighth/Ninth Aves., 212-255-9174, chelseamewsguesthouse.com, cash only)* is an all-male, clothing-optional guest house.

Arts & Entertainment:

Chelsea is the commercial art gallery center of New York, and your best bet to appreciate the almost overwhelming scene here is to simply wander up and down Chelsea's streets west of Ninth Avenue: you'll probably discover a show opening. Both established, and emerging art collectors have been visiting the **Agora Gallery (9)** *(530 W. 25th St., 10th/11th Aves., 212-226-4151, www.agora-gallery. com; hours: Tu–Sa 11AM–6PM)* since its opening in 1984. It showcases a dynamic range of artists from "around the world and around the corner." **The Kitchen (10)** *(512 W. 19th St., Tenth/Eleventh Aves., 212-255-5793, www.the kitchen.org; hours: Tu–F 12PM–6PM, Sa 11AM–6PM)* is another big Chelsea draw, offering a gallery and a constantly changing series of live performance and video art. The **Museum at the Fashion Institute of Technology (11)** *(Seventh Ave. at W. 27th St., 212-217-4558, www.fitnyc. edu; hours: Tu–F 12PM–8PM, Sa 10AM–5PM)*, an exhibition space attached to this famous powerhouse of New York design, offers immaculately curated shows related to fashion and its social impact. Located in a 20,000-square-foot warehouse, the **Gagosian Gallery (12)** *(555 W. 24th St., Tenth/Eleventh Aves., 212-741-1111, www.gagosian. com; hours: Tu–Sa 10AM–6PM)* showcases a wide variety of contemporary artists, from Pablo Picasso to Bob Dylan to Jeff Koons. The **Rubin Museum of Art (13)** *(150 W. 17th St. at 7th Ave., 212-620-5000, www.rmanyc.org; hours: M 11AM–5PM, W 11AM–9PM, Th 11AM–5PM, F 11AM–10PM, Sa–Su 11AM–6PM)* is dedicated to art of the Himalayas and surrounding areas. Chelsea is more than just art galleries, however, and if you love contemporary dance, the **Joyce Theater (14)** *(175 Eighth Ave. at W. 19th St.,*

212-691-9740, www.joyce.org) is not only one of the most beautiful theaters, but also offers some of the most innovative programming, such as the Ballet Hispanico, Savion Glover, and Pilobolus.

PLACES TO EAT & DRINK
Where to Eat:

For rustic Italian, **La Bottega (15) ($$)** *(Maritime Hotel, 363 W. 16th St. at Ninth Ave., 212-242-4300, www.the maritimehotel.com; hours: Su–Th 7AM–12AM, F–Sa 7AM– 1AM)* is a good bet. On warm days, laze afternoons away with Italian cocktails and some small plates of food on the outdoor patio. If you're over by the **Starrett-Lehigh Building (4)** or checking out galleries, **Bottino (16) ($$$)** *(246 Tenth Ave., W. 24th/W. 25th Sts., 212-206-6766, www.bottino nyc.com; hours: M 6PM–10:30PM, Tu–Sa 12PM–3:30PM and 6PM–10:30PM, Su 5:30PM–9:30PM)* is a beautifully minimalist place to enjoy a drink or enjoy a Tuscan meal in one of its two dining rooms. **La Lunchonette (17) ($$)** *(130 Tenth Ave. at W. 18th St., 212-675-0342; hours: M–F 11:30AM– 3:30PM and 5:30PM–11PM, Sa–Su 11AM–3:30PM and 5:30PM–11PM)* offers delicious French bistro food in a long, low, and intimate setting. You won't pay much for the delicious Puerto Rican lunch counter chow at **La Taza de Oro (18) ($)** *(96 Eighth Ave. at 15th St., 212- 243-9946; hours: M–Sa 6AM–10:30PM)* . . . but you may need to let your pants out if you dine there too often. **The Red Cat (19) ($$)** *(227 Tenth Ave., 23rd/24th Sts., 212-242-1122, www.redcatrestaurants.com; hours: brunch Sa–Su 11:30AM–2:45PM, lunch W–F 12PM–2:30PM, dinner M–Sa 5PM–11PM, Su 5PM–10PM)* offers innovative American-inspired cuisine that is deliciously simple, yet bold. Try **Better Burger NYC (20) ($)** *(178 Eighth Ave. at W. 19th St., 212-989-6688, www.betterburgernyc.com; hours: Su–Th 11AM–11PM, F–Sa 11AM–12AM)* for air-baked, antibiotic-free burgers and fries. The health-minded fast-food spot also serves healthier hot dogs. **Hale and Hearty Soups (21) ($)** *(Chelsea Market, 75 Ninth Ave., W. 15th/W. 16th Sts., 212-255-2433, www.haleandhearty.com; hours: M–F 7:30AM–8PM, Sa–Su 11AM–7PM)* offers an excellent selection of soups (and breakfast) daily. Hop aboard the **Frying Pan (22) ($)** *(Pier 66, near 26th St. & West Side Highway, 212-362-4453, www.fryingpan.com; hours: May–Oct. daily 12PM–12AM)*, an old boat-turned-bar and grill, that's docked on a railroad car barge at Pier 66, for traditional burgers and fries.

Bars & Nightlife:

For drinks, **The Half King Bar (23)** *(505 W. 23rd St. at Tenth Ave., 212-462-4300, www.thehalfking.com; hours: breakfast or lunch 11AM–4PM, dinner 4PM–12AM, late night M–Sa 12AM–2AM, brunch Sa–Su 9AM–4PM)*, part-owned by author Sebastian Junger, offers perfect pub-grub and pints. **Peter McManus (24)** *(152 Seventh Ave. at W. 19th St., 212-929-9691; hours: M–Sa 11AM–4AM, Su 12PM–4AM)* is a classic no-frills Irish bar, and the **Trailer Park Lounge (25)** *(271 W. 23rd St., Seventh/Eighth Aves., 212-463-8000, www.trailerparklounge.com; hours: daily from 12PM–2AM)* has some frills—if you consider white-trash kitsch a frill. While somewhat isolated from the rest of the city, the far West Side maintains a vibrant—if hidden—nightlife. Tucked beneath New York's celebrated Chelsea Market (36), **The Tippler (26)** *(425 West 15th St., Ninth/Tenth Aves., 212-206-0000, www.thetippler.com, hours: Su–Th*

4PM-2AM, F–Sa 4PM-4AM) inhabits a historic space that had not been revealed to the public in over 100 years. Classic architectural elements—brick archways, industrial undertones including locally salvaged artifacts like reclaimed water tower wood and train rails from the nearby highline enhance the welcoming interior. Stop in for inventive cocktails, craft beer, and esoteric wines in a lively yet relaxed atmosphere. A more posh "scene" can be found at the **Penthouse at the Park (27)** *(118 10th Ave., 17th/18th Sts., 212-352-3313, www.theparknyc.com; hours: F–Sa 12AM–4AM)*, which has a rooftop patio bar and a stunning garden area.

WHERE TO SHOP

If you've got the right body (and wallet), Comme des Garçons **(28)** *(520 W. 22nd St., Tenth/Eleventh Aves., 212-604-9200; hours: M–Sa 11AM–7PM, Su 12PM–6PM)* has those minimalist pants and dresses you desire, and Diane von Furstenberg **(29)** *(874 Washington St., 13th/14th Sts., 646-486-4800, www.dvf.com; hours: M–Sa 11AM–7PM, Su 12PM–6PM)* will outfit you in the legendary fashion maven's iconic designs. Housing Works **(30)** *(143 W. 17th St., Sixth/Seventh Aves., 718-838-5050, www.housingworks. org; hours: M–F 10AM–7PM, Sa 10AM–6PM, Su 12PM–6PM)* offers excellent thrifting for a good cause. Fittingly located in the art-centric Chelsea is the bookstore 192 Books **(31)** *(192 10th Ave., at 21st St., 212-255-4022, www.192 books.com; hours: daily 11AM–7PM)*. It often presents art exhibitions coinciding with books relating to the art theme or the artists themselves. For a trip down memory lane, head to Authentiques Past and Present **(32)** *(255 W. 18th St., 7th/8th Aves., 212-675-2179, www.fab-stuff.*

com; hours: W–Sa 12PM–6PM, Su 1PM–6PM)—a treasure trove of antiques—including vintage postcards, barware, kitchen items, and lamps. If you're a jazz fan, the Jazz Record Center (33) (236 W. 26th St., Seventh/Eighth Aves., 8th floor, 212-675-4480, www.jazzrecordcenter.com; hours: M–Sa 10AM–6PM, Th 10AM–9:30PM) is a real find. Check out the Angel Street Thrift Shop (34) (118 W. 17th St., 6th/7th Aves., 212-229-0546, angelstreetthrift.org; hours: M–F 11AM–7PM, Sa 10AM–7PM, Su 12PM–5PM) for more valuable finds from furniture to fashion. The shop's proceeds go toward programs for New Yorkers with substance abuse, mental illness, and HIV/AIDS. One of New York's finest vintage shops, the Family Jewels Vintage Clothing (35) (130 W. 23rd St., 6th/7th Aves., 212-633-6020, www.family jewelsnyc.com; hours: W–Sa 11AM–8PM, Su–Tu 11AM–7PM) stocks designer fashions and accessories. One of the neighborhood's gems, Chelsea Market (36) (75 Ninth Ave., W. 15th/W. 16th Sts., 212-652-2110, www.chelseamarket. com; hours: M–Sa 7AM–10PM, Su 8AM–9PM) is home to many artisanal food producers and restaurants. The market, which sits underneath the High Line (5) (see page 104) is a great place for a quick bite or to pack a picnic.

WHERE TO STAY

While the Chelsea Hotel (1) ($$-$$$$) (see page 103) status is in flux, check out the Chelsea Lodge (37) ($) (318 W. 20th St., Eighth/Ninth Aves., 212-243-4499, www. chelsealodge.com), set in a discreet brownstone building. The Manhattan West Hotel (38) ($$) (303 W. 30th St. at Eighth Ave., 212-244-7300, www.manhattanwesthotel. com) offers simple, modern rooms at reasonable prices.

GARMENT DISTRICT

🅐🅒🅔 *to 34th St.;* ❶❷❸ *to 34th St.-Penn Station;* 🅑🅓🅕🅜 🅝🅞🅠🅡 *to 34th St.*

● SNAPSHOT ●

Slightly south of **Times Square** *(approximately W. 28th to W. 40th Sts./Sixth to Eighth Aves.)* lies the Garment District, containing New York's clothing industry. You'll know you're there when you stumble upon racks of clothes being wheeled across the street. Take a peek— you may be looking at next season's high fashion. You'll also find button, fur, and fabric shops dotted around this neighborhood.

PLACES TO SEE
Landmarks:

The biggest store of all, of course, is **Macy's (44)** *(151 W. 34th St., Broadway/Seventh Ave., 212-695-4400, www.macys.com; hours: M–F 9AM–9:30PM, Sa 10AM–9:30PM, Su 11AM–8:30PM).* From designer clothes to pepper grinders and restaurants, this block-sized megastore's got it all. Right opposite is **Herald Square (45)** *(1328 Broadway at 34th St.),* and at its southern end **Greeley Square (46)**, which offers chairs in which to take a breather, when you manage to find an open one. Another big landmark in the area is **Madison Square Garden (47)** *(Seventh Ave.,*

W. 31st/W. 33rd Sts., 212-465-6741, www.thegarden. com). As New Yorkers love to point out, it isn't on Madison, it isn't a square, and it isn't a garden, but otherwise it lives up to its reputation as "the world's most famous arena," home to pro basketball and hockey games, circuses, concerts, and more. Be warned: basketball tickets for the New York Knicks are almost impossible to get, though you can try the box office on game day. Below the ugly hulk of MSG lies **Penn Station (48)** *(Seventh Ave., W. 31st/33rd Sts.)* an equally unlovely station, built in the '60s on the ashes of the fabulous old station, whose demolition sparked the landmark movement. Fortunately, plans are afoot to restore the magnificent McKim, Mead & White **General Post Office (49)** *(Eighth Ave., W. 31st/W. 33rd Sts.)* nearby, with its massive columned facade, into the new arrival terminal for Penn Station, which will also include links to JFK airport.

WHERE TO SHOP

The Garment District has many (albeit rather pedestrian) shopping options. **Victoria's Secret (50)** *(1328 Broadway at 34th St., 212-356-8380, www.victoriassecret.com; hours: M–Tu, Sa 9AM–9:30PM, W 9AM–7PM, Th 10AM–6PM, F 7AM–10PM, Su 10AM–9PM),* that arch purveyor of sexy lingerie, has its flagship store right here in the Garment District, with a huge range of items available. Try **H & M (51)** *(1328 Broadway, at 34th St., 646-473-1165, www. hm.com; hours: M–Sa 9AM–10PM, Su 10AM–9PM)* for on-trend, affordable clothes.

🅐🅒🅔 *to 42nd St.-Port Authority Bus Terminal;*
🅝🅠🅡 ❶❷❸ ❼ 🅢 *to 42nd St.-Times Square*

● **SNAPSHOT** ●

TOP PICK!

In classic New York style, the city's most famous square, ★**TIMES SQUARE** is not a square at all, but the arrowhead where two major thoroughfares—Broadway and Seventh Avenue—meet. In 1905 it acquired its modern name when *The New York Times* newspaper moved uptown to occupy the spot, marking the occasion with a massive New Year's Eve fireworks display that ushered in the role for which the site has become famous. *The New York Times* subsequently decamped to 43rd Street and the old building quickly became a peculiarly American icon as its owners realized it was worth more as a giant billboard than a functioning building. (Today, the area is so well associated with advertising that the Landmarks Commission, in a bizarre ruling, actually requires new buildings in the area to smother their facades with billboards.) With *The New York Times* as its commercial linchpin, theater houses flocked uptown, and by the early 1920s the area had become the city's principal theatrical neighborhood, followed a few years later by the movie theaters. The movie theaters have by and large all gone, but Times Square remains New York's theatrical center, with all the major theaters concentrated on or just off Broadway from the 40s through the 50s. More than 100 years from when the first theaters were built, it's still the place to come to see the latest drama, musical, or revue. Times Square is, of course, famous for its sleaze, and while pockets of XXX-related businesses still linger on (generally west of Eighth Avenue), the past ten years or so have seen a major face-lift and a return—hotly debated by some New Yorkers—to a more family-friendly environment.

PLACES TO SEE
Landmarks:
The New York Times, in its various guises, still dominates the area. Aside from the **New York Times Building (original) (52)** *(1 Times Square, W. 42nd St., Broadway/Seventh Ave.),* now most famous as the tower from which the New Year's Eve glass ball drops, there's the chateau-style **New York Times Building (53)** *(217-247 W. 43rd St., Seventh/Eighth Aves.)* that replaced it nearby, which *The New York Times* vacated for a fancy new skyscraper in 2007. **NASDAQ MarketSite (54)** *(Broadway and 43rd St., www.nasdaq.com/reference/marketsite_about.stm)* represents Times Square's visual cacophony in a manner both elegant and extreme. It's the physical face of the electronic NASDAQ stock market, the largest of its kind in the world. The cylindrical tower is wrapped in

an amazing seven-story LED video screen which displays financial news as it breaks, as well as (this being Times Square) advertising. The building also hosts market events, and contains a broadcast studio. A spate of remarkable skyscrapers went up in Times Square over the last decade, including the **Reuters Building (55)** *(3 Times Square, NE corner of Broadway)* and the **4 Times Square (56)** *(4 Times Square, 42nd/43rd Sts.)*, with its elegant stepped facade, which housed Condé Nast until the publication's recent move to 1 World Trade. Times Square was also famous in its day for what was known as Tin Pan Alley, or the pop music business. The center of it was the **Brill Building (57)** *(1619 Broadway at 49th St.)*, where Phil Spector—among many others—worked. It's in the heart of **Music Row (58)** *(48th St., Sixth/Seventh Aves.)* where you'll find plenty of small stores selling guitars and other musical equipment. The **Time & Life Building (59)** *(1271 Sixth Ave., 50th/51st Sts.)* has one of the best public lobbies in the city, complete with works of art.

Arts & Entertainment:

Times Square is all about theater, of course, and the one with the most spectacular Beaux Arts facade is the **Lyceum Theatre (60)** *(149-157 W. 45th St., Sixth/Seventh Aves.)*, which also has a great marble lined interior, complete with murals. Bette Davis and Angela Lansbury, among other stars, performed here. The **Ed Sullivan Theater (61)** *(1697-1699 Broadway, W. 53rd/*

W. 54th Sts.) home to David Letterman's *Late Show,* is also a great old theater and a good place to catch stars popping in and out for the early afternoon tapings of the show. (For tickets, apply at the CBS website, www.cbs. com, or visit the theater Monday–Friday, 9:30AM–12PM, weekends 10AM–6PM.) The **Winter Garden Theater (62)** *(1634-1646 Broadway, W. 50th/W. 51st Sts., www. wintergarden-theater.com)* has been home to Al Jolson and the *Ziegfeld Follies* in its past, and now is best known as the place where *Cats* became Broadway's longest-running show. The **Al Hirschfeld Theater (63)** *(302-314 W. 45th St., Eighth/Ninth Aves.),* named after the famed *New York Times* caricaturist, has one of the most knock-out interiors of all, which alone is worth the price of a ticket. Tickets for these and all other Broadway theaters are most easily purchased online from various ticket brokers, though it's possible to purchase a limited number of day-of-performance tickets from their box offices. Another good place to buy day-of-performance tickets, and at discounts of up to 50%, is the **TKTS Booth (64)** *(center island of W. 47th St., Broadway/Seventh Aves., www.tdf.org)* in Duffy Square. For more information on where to buy tickets and what's on, visit the indispensable **Times Square Visitors Center (65)** *(1560 Broadway W 46th/W 47th Sts., www.timessquarenyc. org, daily 8AM–8PM).* For non-theatrical entertainment, there's **Carnegie Hall (66)** *(154 W. 57th St. at Seventh Ave., 212-247-7800, www.carnegiehall.com),* worth the pilgrimage alone to admire its handsome facade. It also has an excellent performance space beneath it, **Zankel Hall (66)** *(see Carnegie Hall website above for details).*

For great jazz, cabaret, readings, and more, there's **Town Hall (67)** *(123 W. 43rd St., Broadway/Sixth Ave., 212-840-2824, www.the-townhall-nyc.org)*. If you want something a little different, try **Madame Tussauds New York (68)** *(234 W. 42nd St., Seventh/Eighth Aves., 212-512-9600, www.nycwax.com; hours: Su–Th 10AM–8PM, F–Sa 10AM–10PM)*, where Ozzy Osbourne, Derek Jeter, and other waxen luminaries await. Walk west to enjoy the pleasures of the waterfront. **Hudson River Park (8)** *(Hudson River to West Side Hwy., Battery Park City to 59th St., www.hudsonriverpark.org)*, has lovely restored piers, tennis courts, a skate park, and more. Or take a ride on one of the great tourist pleasures: the **Circle Line (69)** *(W. 42nd St. at Pier 83, Hudson River, 212-563-3200, www.circleline42.com)*. This is a three-hour boat tour around Manhattan, passing underneath all its many bridges, with funny and knowledgeable tour guides who'll turn you into an instant Manhattan expert. Nearby is the **Intrepid Sea-Air-Space Museum (70)** *(W. 46th St. at Pier 86, Hudson River, 212-245-0072, www.intrepidmuseum.org; hours: April 1–Oct 31 M–F 10AM–5PM, Sa–Su 10AM–6PM; Nov. 1–March 31 Tu–Su 10AM–5PM)*, set on the massive bulk of the old *Intrepid* aircraft carrier and full of interactive amusements, two submarines, numerous jet engines, and, as of summer 2012, the Space Shuttle Orbiter Enterprise. Pick up a tour of *New York TV and Movie Sites* from **On Location Tours (71)** *(meeting place near Broadway & 51st St., 212-683-2027, www.screentours.com; call in advance for tickets)* leaving daily at 11AM. You'll see favorite city hotspots from *Seinfeld, Friends, How I Met Your Mother,* and more. The company also offers *Sex and the City* and *Sopranos* tours. Visit **Discovery Times Square** *(226 W. 44th St., Seventh/Eighth Aves., 866-987-9692, www. discoverytsx.com, Su–Tu 10AM–7PM, W–Th 10AM–8PM, F–Sa 10AM–9PM)* for ever-changing immersive exhibits from Harry Potter™ to Pompeii to King Tut.

Kids:

Times Square is now famously family- and kid-friendly since Disney moved in and forced the grittier elements out. Some New Yorkers carp at this, but one result has been the restoration of two magnificent theaters, the **New Amsterdam Theatre (72)** *(214 W. 42nd St., Seventh/Eighth Aves., www.new-amsterdam-theatre.com)* and the **New Victory Theater (73)** *(209 W. 42nd St., Seventh/Eighth Aves., 646-223-3010, www.newvictory.org)*. The New Amsterdam first premiered the eternally running smash *The Lion King*, while the New Victory is dedicated to children's theatrical shows by visiting companies. There's also **Madame Tussauds (68)** *(see page 118)*, and a gargantuan branch of Toys "R" Us (74) (which will be closing in February) *(1514 Broadway, W. 44th/W. 45th Sts., 646-366-8800, www.toysrus.com; hours: Su–Th 10AM–10PM, F 10AM–11PM, Su 9AM–11PM)* that features a 60-foot-high Ferris wheel, a 20-foot-high T-Rex, plus a LEGO model of the Empire State Building. If your kids are adventurous, you can check out the world of weird and bizarre relics at **Ripley's Believe It or Not! Odditorium (75)** *(234 W. 42nd St., 7th/8th Aves., 212-398-3133, www.ripleysnewyork.com; hours: daily 9AM–1AM)*. Marvel at the unusual artifacts such as shrunken heads, a six-legged cow, and a section of the Berlin Wall.

PLACES TO EAT & DRINK
Where to Eat:

If you're going to a show and in a hurry, there's always **Restaurant Row (76)** *(W. 46th St., Eighth/Ninth Aves.)*. Just let the server know you're heading to a show. Since the restaurants cater to the theater crowd, they know how to put food on the table quickly. **B. Smith's (77) ($$$)** *(320 W. 46th St. at Eighth Ave., 212-315-1100; www. bsmith.com; hours: M 5PM–10PM, Tu, Th 5PM–11PM, W 11:30AM–11PM, F 5PM–12:30AM, Sa 11:30AM–12:30AM, Su 11:30AM–10PM)* serves the owner's spins on American cuisine with Southern influences. **Brazil Brazil Churrascaria (78) ($)** *(328 W. 46th St., Eighth/Ninth Aves., 212-957-4300, www.brazil46.com; hours: daily 12PM–12AM)* offers tasty steaks in a bright atmosphere with a garden. Italian restaurant **Orso (79) ($$-$$$)** *(322 W. 46th St., Eighth/Ninth Aves., 212-489-7212, www.orsorestaurant. com; hours: M, Tu, Th, F 12PM–11:45PM; W, Sa, Su 11:30AM–11:45PM)* is one of the best places on the strip and often stuffed with Broadway stars. If you have time, or if you're looking for a more relaxed post-theater meal, venture west to **Hell's Kitchen** *(40s and 50s west of Eighth Ave.)*, a neighborhood full of great bars and restaurants. There's **Kodama Sushi (80) ($)** *(301 W. 45th St., Eighth/Ninth Aves., 212-582-8065, hours: M–F 12PM–11PM, Sa 12:30PM–11PM, Su 5PM–10PM)* for no-frills sushi in a no-frills space, or low-cost and delicious kosher Israeli food at **Azuri Café (81) ($)** *(465 W. 51st St., Ninth/Tenth Aves., 212-262-*

2920, *www.azuricafe.com; hours: Su–Th 10:30AM–9PM, F 10:30AM–4PM).* You won't find many locals at New York's famous **Carnegie Deli (82) ($–$$)** *(854 Seventh Ave. at 55th St., 212-757-2245, www.carnegiedeli.com; hours: daily 6:30AM–2AM)* but you will find some big sandwiches. Treat yourself to a sandwich and baked treat at locally-loved (and owned) chainlet **Amy's Bread (83) ($)** *(672 Ninth Ave., 46th/47th Sts., 212-977-2670, www.amysbread.com; hours: M–Tu 7:30AM–10PM, W–F 7:30AM–11PM, Sa 8AM–11PM, Su 8AM–10PM).* If you have a hankering for some serious barbeque, head to **Daisy May's BBQ USA (84) ($)** *(623 11th Ave., at 46th St., 212-977-1500, www.daisymaysbbq.com; hours: M 11AM–9PM, Tu–F 11AM–10PM, Sa 12PM–10PM, Su 12PM–9PM)* for savory, sweet, and downright delicious fixin's.

Bars & Nightlife:

Pulse Karaoke Lounge (85) *(135 W. 41st. St., Sixth Ave./ Broadway, 212-278-0090, www.pulsekaraoke.com; hours: M–Th 6PM–2AM, F–Sa 6PM–4AM),* features over 85,000 songs in up to 14 different languages. Special lighting and even gaming stations are available. It's sometimes closed for private parties, so check the website for specific opening times. You'll find many bars lining 9th Avenue. Check out the **Mercury Bar (86)** *(659 9th Ave., 45th/46th Sts., 212-262-7755, www.mercurybarnyc.com; hours: M–F 11:30AM–4AM, Sa–Su 10:30AM–4AM)* to enjoy sports on its big-screen TVs, and its friendly bartenders who will mix up any drink you like!

WHERE TO SHOP

Times Square and its environs is not the most restful area to shop, but many tourists find the bustling **M&M's World (87)** *(1600 Broadway, at 48th St., 212-295-3850, www.mmsworld.com; hours: daily 9AM–12AM)* a must-stop for their M&M fix. You can create your very own mix of colored candies by using the candy dispensers, and see any of the new flavors on the market. Unique to this New York location, is the 17-foot Green M&M's girl posing as none other than Lady Liberty. A sweet time can be had by all at **Hershey's Times Square (88)** *(1593 Broadway, at 48th St., 212-581-9100, www.hersheys.com; hours: daily 9AM–12AM)*. The store celebrates Hershey candies—and you! Visitors can actually see their names go up in lights over Broadway. The **Hell's Kitchen Flea Market (89)** *(W. 39th St. 9th/10th Aves., 212-243-5343, www.hellskitchenfleamarket.com; hours: Sa–Su 9AM–5PM)* is a great place to ferret out a bargain, whether it's a piece of retro clothing or a deco coffee pot, though real bargain hunters get there early!

WHERE TO STAY

Staying at the **New York Marriott Marquis Times Square (90) ($$$)** *(1535 Broadway, W. 45th/W. 46th Sts., 212-398-1900, www.nymarriottmarquis.com)* hardly feels like being in New York at all, with its L.A.-style valet parking at street level (you have to take an elevator up to reception), and its dizzying James Bond-style central atrium rising 49 floors; however, it's a real trip staying here, and the views from its revolving bar/restaurant are amazing. **The Muse (91) ($$$)** *(130 W. 46th St., Sixth/Seventh Aves., 212-485-2400, www.themusehotel. com)*, a Kimpton Hotel, is a luxury hotel that serves up plenty of offbeat visual treats. If you're here for the theater, there's no more convenient place to stay.

chapter 5

FLATIRON DISTRICT & GRAMERCY
MIDTOWN & MURRAY HILL

FLATIRON DISTRICT & GRAMERCY MIDTOWN & MURRAY HILL

Places to See:

1. Madison Square Park
2. Flatiron Building
3. New York Life Insurance Company Building
4. The Players
5. National Arts Club
6. Theodore Roosevelt Birthplace
7. 69th Regiment Armory
8. Augustus Saint-Gaudens Park
28. EMPIRE STATE BUILDING ★
29. Chrysler Building
30. ROCKEFELLER CENTER ★
31. NBC
32. ST. PATRICK'S CATHEDRAL ★
33. Radio City Music Hall
34. Lever House
35. Seagram Building
36. Bryant Park
37. New York Public Library
38. GRAND CENTRAL TERMINAL ★
39. Tudor City
40. United Nations Headquarters
41. The Ford Foundation Building
42. MUSEUM OF MODERN ART (MoMA) ★
43. Eden Gallery
44. Paley Center for Media
45. Morgan Library & Museum
46. Scandinavia House
47. Onassis Cultural Center
48. Sony Wonder Technology Lab

Places to Eat & Drink:

10. Craft
11. City Bakery
12. Shake Shack
13. dévi
14. L'Express
15. Eleven Madison Park
16. 71 Irving Place Coffee & Tea Bar
17. Bamiyan
18. Tavern on Third
19. Flatiron Lounge
50. Burger Heaven
51. Dishes
52. Cosi
53. Alcala
54. Morton's, The Steakhouse

★ Top Picks

Where to Shop:

Where to Stay:

FLATIRON DISTRICT & GRAMERCY

🄵 🄼 *to 14th St. or 23rd St.;* 🄻 🄽 🅀 🄿 ❹ ❺ ❻
to 14th St.-Union Square; ❻ *to 23rd St. or 28th St.;*
🄽 🅁 *to 23rd St. or 28th St.*

● SNAPSHOT ●

Today, these districts are alike in both being highly "respectable," thriving neighborhoods, full of shops and museums. However, not so long ago the Flatiron District (roughly 14th to 29th Streets between Fifth and Park Avenues), and its main public space, Madison Square Park, was a raggedy, crime-ridden sister to neighboring Gramercy Park, which had largely retained its slumbering sense of wealthy calm since the 19th century. A huge face-lift to Madison Square Park and the surrounding areas put an end to this disparity, and now both are essential places on any visitor's itinerary.

PLACES TO SEE
Landmarks:

Like Union Square Park nearby, **Madison Square Park (1)** *(23rd to 26th Sts., Fifth Ave. to Madison Ave.)* was transformed from a drug-plagued place to one where crowds sit, eating lunch during the day, or looking at art exhibits and listening to music on summer nights, thanks to the efforts of the Madison Square Park conservancy *(www.madisonsquarepark.org for details).*

The park has several claims to fame, first as the likely site of the country's first baseball team, the New York Knickerbockers, founded by Alexander Cartwright in 1845, and also as the site of the original Madison Square Garden, long since transferred north to its current site above Penn Station. The two most notable buildings are the **Flatiron Building (2)** *(175 Fifth Ave., 22nd/23rd Sts.)*, which gives the neighborhood its name, and the **New York Life Insurance Company Building (3)** *(51 Madison Ave., 26th/27th Sts.)*. A gorgeous wedge-shaped 22-story slice of Renaissance terra cotta completed in 1903, the **Flatiron Building (2)** gained its name because it was shaped like a clothing iron. At the time, the building's high-rise steel structure was innovative, and it became an instant landmark at the northern end of what was known as "Ladies Mile," the city's most important shopping area. The other great neighborhood edifice, the **New York Life Insurance Company Building (3)** was designed by Cass Gilbert, the same architect who built the Woolworth Building. This lovely 40-story limestone building was built on the site of the original Madison Square Garden. Gramercy Park—unlike Madison Square Park's open-to-all democracy—is based on the English form of a private garden in the center of a square and is only open to residents who have a key, an infinitely prized status object among local residents. Just because you can't get in doesn't mean you shouldn't gaze at the surrounding buildings: there's **The Players (4)** *(16 Gramercy Park S., Park Ave. S./Irving Pl.,*

212-475-6116, www.theplayers nyc.org), a beautiful Greek Revival town house once owned by famous actor Edwin Booth (his brother shot Lincoln). It is now a private club for men and women in the arts and business. Next door is another famous club, the **National Arts Club (5)** *(15 Gramercy Park S., www. nationalartsclub.org)*, in Gothic

Revival style, where in a suitable boozy atmosphere artists and writers still disport themselves amid walls displaying their art.

Arts & Entertainment:

If you like your museums dimly lit and uncrowded, the wonderful **Theodore Roosevelt Birthplace (6)** *(28 E. 20th St., Broadway/Park Ave. S., 212-260-1616, www.nps.gov/ thrb; hours: Tu–Sa 9AM–5PM)* is for you. A national historic site (though the original building was demolished in 1916), uniformed Federal Rangers offer guided tours of the building's period rooms. Much more modern, at least in spirit, is the **69th Regiment Armory (7)** *(68 Lexington Ave., E. 25th/E. 26th Sts., 646-424-5500, www.sixtyninth.net/armory.html)*, host to the original 1913 Armory Show, where Cubism and other shocking European phenomena were first unveiled for the American public. Its vast 27,000-square-foot space is host to a number of important arts and antiques fairs during the year.

Kids:

This isn't the most child-friendly of Manhattan neighborhoods, but there's a lovely playground in the Gramercy Park area called the **Augustus Saint-Gaudens Park (8)** *(19th St. at Second Ave.)*. Whether you're an adult or a kid, you'll love Books of Wonder (9) *(18 W. 18th St., Fifth/Sixth Aves., 212-989-3270, www.booksof wonder.com; hours: M–Sa 10AM–7PM, Su 11AM–6PM)*, which stocks childhood classics from *Winnie the Pooh* to *Harry Potter*. It also offers frequent author readings and signings.

PLACES TO EAT & DRINK
Where to Eat:

Owned by Chef Tom Colicchio—of "Top Chef" fame—**Craft (10) ($$$)** *(43 E. 19th St., Broadway/Park Ave. S., 212-780-0880, www.craftrestaurant.com; hours: Su–Th 5:30PM–10PM, F–Sa 5:30PM–11PM)* is an amazingly minimalist space with simple food. **City Bakery (11) ($)** *(3 W. 18th St., Fifth/Sixth Aves., 212-366-1414, www.thecitybakery.com; hours: M–F 7:30AM–7PM, Sa 8AM–7PM, Su 10AM–6PM, closes half an hour earlier in summer)* is a neighborhood standard famous for great pastries and even better hot chocolate. If you're in Madison Square Park, don't miss **Shake Shack (12) ($)** *(S. Side*

Park, near Madison Ave./23rd St., 212-889-6600, www.shake shack.com; daily 11AM–11PM), which serves up stellar burgers to go with its namesake treat. Over at **dévi (13) ($$)** *(8 E.*

18th St., Broadway/Fifth Ave., 212-691-2100, *www.devinyc.com*; hours: M–Th 11:30AM–3PM, 6PM–10PM, F 11:30AM–10:30PM, Sa 12PM–11PM, Su 12PM–10PM) there's wonderful Indian food served in a brightly lit, colorful atmosphere. French bistro **L'Express (14) ($$)** *(249 Park Ave. S. at 20th St., 212-254-5858, www.lexpressnyc.com; hours: daily, open 24 hours)*, a locals' favorite, hums 24 hours a day. For an upscale (read: pricey) dining experience, head to **Eleven Madison Park (15) ($$$$)** *(11 Madison Ave. at 24th St., 212-889-0905, www.elevenmadisonpark.com; hours: lunch Th–Sa 12PM-1PM, dinner M–Su 5:30PM-10PM)*, which features French tasting menus from world-famous chef Daniel Humm served in a high-ceilinged Art Deco space. For tasty sandwiches and delicious baked goods, try **71 Irving Place Coffee & Tea Bar (16) ($$)** *(71 Irving Place, E. 18th/19th Sts., 212-995-5252, www.irvingfarm.com; hours: M–F 7AM–10PM, Sa–Su 8AM–10PM)*. If you've never had Afghan cuisine, you don't know what you're missing. Head to one of the city's best Persian restaurants, **Bamiyan (17) ($–$$)** *(358 3rd Ave., at 26th St., 212-481-3232, www.bamiyan.com; hours: M–Th 4:30PM–11PM, F 4:30PM–11PM, Sa 11AM–1AM, Su 11AM–11PM)*, for delicious basmati rice dishes, lamb and chicken kabobs, mild curries, and a variety of dumplings. Don't miss the "Kadu" appetizer—pumpkin turnovers that will melt in your mouth.

Bars & Nightlife:

The **Tavern on Third (18)** (*380 Third Ave. at 27th St., 212-300-4046, www.tavernonthird.com; hours: daily 11:30AM–4AM*) is a spacious, comfortable sports bar with self-pour tap tables, an excellent happy hour, and good pub grub. Those passionate about well-poured cocktails would

do well to spend an evening at **Flatiron Lounge (19)** (*37 W. 19th St., 5th/6th Aves., 212-727-7741; www.flatiron lounge.com; hours: M–W 4PM–2AM, Th 4PM–3AM, F 4PM–4AM, Sa 5PM–4AM, Su 5PM–2AM*). The bartenders mix stunning drinks (in looks, taste, and, at times, knockout power).

WHERE TO SHOP

Like the raffish English gent aesthetic? You can't go wrong shopping at **Paul Smith (20)** (*108 Fifth Ave. at 16th St., 212-627-9770, www.paulsmith.co.uk; hours: M–W, F–Sa 11AM–7PM, Th 11AM–8PM, Su 12PM–6PM*). Smith's tailored suits, famous striped socks and shirts, and super-cool shoes can't be beat. If you're a music lover, **Academy Records (21)** (*12 W. 18th St., Fifth/Sixth Aves., 212-242-3000, www.academy-records. com; hours: daily 11AM–7PM*) has an amazing jazz and classical collection in both vinyl and CD format in a browser-friendly environment. **Fishs**

Eddy (22) *(889 Broadway at E. 19th St., 212-420-9020, www.fishseddy.com; hours: M–Th 9AM–9PM, F–Sa 9AM–10PM, Su 10AM–8PM)* is a mini-chain that offers irresistible china and glassware from overstocked corporations, factories, and out-of-business restaurants. They also stock fun designs created just for the store. Skip out on boring souvenirs. Put your money toward the NYC-themed dishes instead. ABC Carpet & Home (23) *(888 Broadway at E. 19th St., 212-473-3000, www.abchome.com; hours: M–W, F–Sa 10AM–7PM, Th 10AM–8PM, Su 11AM–6:30PM)* is famous for its huge selection of home furnishings, decorations, and bazaar-like atmosphere.

WHERE TO STAY

Indulge yourself during a stay at the luxurious **Hotel Giraffe (24)** **($$$-$$$$)** *(365 Park Ave. S. at 26th St., 218-685-7700, www.hotelgiraffe.com)*. The design throughout is inspired by the 1920s and '30s, with rich lavish colors and textures creating a sophisticated, yet comfortable setting. Amenities include all the cappuccino, espresso, cookies, and fruit that you can eat all day, a complimentary breakfast buffet, and champagne, wine, and cheese to wind down your day while you listen to live cocktail piano music. Ian Schrager has transformed the **Gramercy Park Hotel (25)** **($$$$)** *(2 Lexington Ave. at 21st St., 212-920-3300, www.gramercypark hotel.com)* into an elegantly modern oasis, combining different styles of furniture, art, and rich colors to create a diverse, sensuous setting. There is a lovely private roof club with a bar and landscaped garden.

MIDTOWN & MURRAY HILL

Ⓑ Ⓓ Ⓕ Ⓜ to 42nd St.-Bryant Park or
47th-50th Sts.-Rockefeller Center; Ⓢ ④ ⑤ ⑥ ⑦ to
Grand Central-42nd St.; Ⓝ Ⓡ Ⓠ to Fifth Ave.-59th
St.; Ⓔ Ⓜ to Fifth Ave.-53rd St.

● SNAPSHOT ●

When visitors think of New York, the first images that
come to mind are usually the iconic ones of its famous
skyscrapers, in all their Deco glory, rising high above
the bustling streets. This is Midtown, the place that for
many—New Yorkers and tourists alike—epitomizes the
city. It's here that Fifth Avenue swells to its most majestic
state. The Empire State Building, Chrysler Building,
Rockefeller Center, and United Nations complex, to
name just a few, ascend skyward, and Radio City Music
Hall, Tiffany's, the Plaza Hotel, Saks, and a host of other
New York institutions made familiar through a million
TV shows and movies, can be found here. It's no wonder that a first-time visitor's impression is
often: *Haven't I seen all this before?* Murray
Hill, a highly fashionable residential area in
lower Midtown, contains some remarkable
buildings (in particular a number of lovely
carriage houses now converted to residences),
as well as restaurants and shops. It's not quite
as electric as Midtown (what is?), but it's
a pleasant and rewarding neighborhood to
venture into if you wish to lower the street
energy for a while.

PLACES TO SEE
Landmarks:

Perhaps the most famous street in the world, **Fifth Avenue** was originally a residential area for the ultra-wealthy, before becoming one of the city's most prestigious commercial strips as the big stores began to move north from 34th Street. Some of the original private mansions were later converted into shops. Cartier Inc. (26) (*653 Fifth Ave. at 52nd St.*), the jewelers, occupies one of the greatest Renaissance mansions on Fifth Avenue. The building is worth seeing, but is undergoing renovation. In the meantime, Cartier is open at Saks Fifth Ave (69) (*see page 147*). Versace (27) (*647 Fifth Ave., 51st/52nd Sts., 212-317-0224, www.versace.com; hours: M–Sa 10AM–7PM, Su 12PM–6PM*) occupies a former Vanderbilt mansion next door. Skyscrapers are

what the neighborhood is famous for, and the ★**EMPIRE STATE BUILDING (28)** (*350 Fifth Ave., 33rd/34th Sts., 212-736-3100, www.esbnyc.com; hours: observatory open 8AM–2AM daily, last elevators go up at 1:15AM*) is the

TOP PICK!

most famous of all, immortalized in films such as *When Harry Met Sally* and *An Affair to Remember*. At 1,250 feet, it beat out the spanking new Chrysler Building for crown of tallest building in the world when it opened in 1931. The sights from its 86th floor viewing level are amazing. (Note that security measures can make for a long wait to get up there.) Admission tickets can also be purchased for the 102nd floor observatory. It may be a touch shorter, but the **Chrysler Building (29)** *(405 Lexington Ave., 42nd/43rd Sts.; hours: M–F 8AM–*

6PM), with its great gargoyles and Deco detailing, is far more romantic and has an infinitely richer public lobby. ★**ROCKEFELLER CENTER (30)** *(Fifth to Sixth Aves., 48th/51st Sts., 212-588-8601, www.rockefellercenter.com)* is a collection of 19 buildings—both office and commercial space—a sunken shopping plaza, and an

TOP PICK!

open-air public plaza, all brilliantly arranged in harmony with each other. Work began in the 1930s and was extended until the early 1950s. The Top of the Rock observation deck offers great views of New York City, and you'll find all kinds of adventures within the complex. **NBC (31)** *(30 Rockefeller Plaza, 49th St., Fifth/Sixth Aves., call 212-664-3700 for tour info, www.nbcstudiotour.com)* is a tenant. There's also good shopping in the plaza above and below, and a wonderful **Rink at Rockefeller Center** for ice-skating, open October to April *(call 212-332-7654 for prices and hours)*. Rockefeller Plaza is the site of New York City's Christmas tree and its celebrity lighting each year.

On a less secular level, there's ★**ST. PATRICK'S CATHEDRAL (32)** *(Fifth Ave., E. 50th/E. 51st Sts., 212-753-2261, www. saintpatrickscathedral.org; hours: daily 6:30AM–8:45PM)* nearby, a Gothic masterpiece where the hush once inside its vast doors makes a lovely contrast to the perpetual bustle outside. It is the largest Gothic Catholic cathedral in North America and seat of the archbishop of the Roman Catholic Archdiocese of New York. **Radio City Music Hall (33)** *(1260 Sixth Ave., W. 50th/W. 51st Sts., 212-247-4777, www.radiocity.com)* remains one of the great architectural and theatrical gems of the city. Today, it's best known for its annual Christmas extravaganza with the high kickin' Rockettes. You can take in its sumptuous interior, without paying for a show, by joining one of the regular behind-the-scenes tours. If you like your architecture modern, a little farther north is the famous **Lever House (34)** *(390 Park Ave., E. 53rd/E. 54th Sts.)*—an International Style stainless steel and glass curtain-walled office building that inspired a million knockoffs. The other classic International Style skyscraper is the **Seagram Building (35)** *(375 Park Ave., E. 52nd/E. 53rd Sts.)*, a sleek, almost ominous, glass and bronze-framed tower designed by Mies van der Rohe and Philip Johnson. Between West 40th and West 42nd Streets on the east side of Sixth Avenue lies **Bryant Park (36)**

(www.bryantpark.org), one of the loveliest public spaces in the city. In warm weather you can pull up a chair, sit on the graveled walkways and enjoy the park's complimentary Wi-Fi. The park is behind the majestic **New York Public Library (37)** *(476 Fifth Ave., W. 42nd to 40th Sts., 917-275-6975, www.nypl.org; call or visit website for hours),* a Beaux Arts masterpiece.

The twin lions, Patience and Fortitude, guard the entrance. The Rose Reading room is worth a visit, and there are usually excellent free exhibitions, too. Eastward lies ★**GRAND CENTRAL TERMINAL (38)** *(E. 42nd to E. 44th Sts., Vanderbilt to Lexington Aves., 212-340-2583, www.grandcentralterminal.com).* One of New York's greatest landmarks, the building was saved from demolition and is now flawlessly restored. The expanded terminal had opened in 1913 and was a hub for area redevelopment until World War II. Years of disrepair followed, until famous New Yorkers like Jacqueline Kennedy Onassis took up the cause. Check out its famous painted ceiling of the constellations. As part of the restoration, there's also a terrific food market on the main level and food court on the lower level *(see pages 144 and 148).* Head toward the East River and you'll encounter **Tudor City (39)** *(E. 40th St. to E. 43rd St., First/Second Aves., www.tudor city.com),* a fascinating 1920s Tudor-style collection of apartment buildings funded by Rockefeller alongside what was once the city's busiest slaughterhouse area. They form an enclave of peace and quiet from busy Second Avenue, and nestling in the middle is a delightful and beautifully maintained public park. Nearby, in high-modern style lies the **United Nations Headquarters (40)** *(E. 42nd to E. 48th Sts., First Ave./FDR Dr., 212-963-8687 for tour info, www.visit.un.org; hours: guided tours M–F 9:15AM–4:15PM, Sa–Su 10AM–4:15PM)*, where you technically leave U.S. soil as you enter. **The Ford Foundation Building (41)** *(321 E. 42nd St., First/Second Aves.)*, with its incredible atrium that is visible from both the street and offices, is arguably the finest postwar building in New York. It's one of the great public spaces in the city and you just know it costs a bundle to keep all those delicate trees alive.

Arts & Entertainment:

Midtown has some excellent museums, including the 630,000-square-foot ★**MUSEUM OF MODERN ART (MoMA) (42)** *(11 W. 53rd St., Fifth/Sixth Aves., 212-708-9400, www.moma.org; hours: Su–M, W, Th, Sa 10:30AM–5:30PM, F 10:30AM–8PM)*. Its white walls and pure spaces are home to a permanent collection by the likes of Matisse, Picasso, Pollock, and Warhol, and it features

TOP PICK!

major exhibitions as well. MoMA "seeks to create a dialogue between the established and the experimental, the past and the present," according to its literature. It's a whopping $25 for adult admission (kids under 16 are free), but few complain once they've seen the incredible collection of visual media inside. It also has arguably the best gift shop of any museum in the city. A bit further to the east and worth a visit is the **Eden Gallery (43)** *(437 Madison Ave., at 50th St., 212-888-0177, www. eden-gallery.com; hours: daily 9AM–9PM)*, which showcases the work of leading Israeli and international artists. This flagship location features a dynamic open space, and its curators focus on exhibiting contemporary, cheerful, and colorful works. The **Paley Center for Media (44)** *(25 W. 52nd St., Fifth/Sixth Aves., 212-621-6800, www. paleycenter.org; hours: W, F–Su 12PM–6PM, Th 12PM–8PM)* provides curated shows, as well as artifacts and screenings from all ages of the American entertainment industry. *(See also page 142.)* The venerable **Morgan Library & Museum (45)** *(225 Madison Avenue, at 36th St., 212-685-0008, www.themorgan.org; hours: Tu–Th 10:30AM–5PM, F 10:30AM–9PM, Sa 10AM–6PM, Su 11AM–6PM)* was the original home of financier J. P. Morgan, and, along with his magnificent library, you can see Morgan's jaw-dropping collection of Italian Renaissance paintings and sculpture. Two other places to view interesting exhibitions: **Scandinavia House (46)** *(58 Park Ave., 37th/38th Sts., 212-779-3587, www. scandinaviahouse.org; hours: Tu–Sa 12PM–6PM)* and the **Onassis Cultural Center (47)** *(645 5th Ave., entrance on 51st St., 212-486-4448, www.onassisusa.org; hours: M–Sa 10AM–6PM)*.

Kids:

The **Paley Center for Media (44)** *(see also page 141)* offers a wonderful series of workshops entitled "Re-creating Radio" *(call 212-621-6600 for details),* in which kids, aged nine and up, collaborate to make an old-fashioned radio serial program, complete with scripts, sound effects, and editing. Afterward, they get to take away a recording of their labors. For the tech-enthusiast among your kids, you can't beat the **Sony Wonder Technology Lab (48)** *(56th St. at Madison Ave., 212-833-8100, http:// wondertechlab.sony.com; reservations are recommended; a limited number of same day tickets are available on a first come first serve basis beginning at 9:30AM Tu–Sa)*—four floors of interactive fun, including a 73-seat HDTV viewing theater, where you and your kids can make music, video, and film clips, explore computers, and much more. The flagship store of **FAO Schwarz (49)** *(767 Fifth Ave., 58th/59th Sts., www.fao.com)* has closed. They are in the process of looking for a less expensive location.

PLACES TO EAT & DRINK
Where to Eat:

For a quick and cheap burger fix, there's **Burger Heaven (50) ($)** (*20 E. 49th St., Fifth/Madison Aves., 212-755-2166, www.burgerheaven.com; hours: M–F 7AM–7:30PM, Sa 8AM–5:45PM, Su 9:30AM–4:30PM*)—rushed, but tasty. For sandwiches, soups, and salads (weekdays only) that are head and shoulders above the average, **Dishes (51) ($)** (*6 E. 45th St., Fifth/Madison Aves., 212-687-5511, www.dishestogo.com; hours: M–F 7AM–5PM*) is the place to go. **Cosi (52) ($)** (*60 E. 56th St., Madison/Park Aves., 212-588-1225, www.getcosi.com; hours: M–F 6:30AM–7PM, Sa–Su 11AM–6PM*) chain of sandwich shops is also a good cheap bet. If you want to splurge more and you like tapas and Basque food, **Alcala (53) ($$)** (*246 E. 44th St., First/Second Aves., 212-370-1866, www.alcala restaurant.com; hours: M–Th 12PM–11PM, F 12PM–12AM, Sa 3:30PM–12AM, Su 5PM–9:30PM*) is excellent. For a serious carnivorous session,

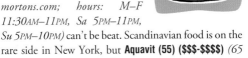

Morton's, The Steakhouse (54) ($$$-$$$$) (*551 Fifth Ave. at 45th St., 212-972-3315, www.mortons.com; hours: M–F 11:30AM–11PM, Sa 5PM–11PM, Su 5PM–10PM*) can't be beat. Scandinavian food is on the rare side in New York, but **Aquavit (55) ($$$-$$$$)** (*65 E. 55th St., Madison/Park Aves., 212-307-7311, www.aquavit.org; lunch M–F 11:45AM–2:30PM; dinner M–Sa*

5:30PM–10:30PM) wows even jaded city palates. The seven-course tasting menu is an escapist pleasure. Be treated to regional Japanese cuisine at **Aburiya Kinnosuke (56) ($$-$$$)** *(213 E. 45th St. at 3rd Ave., 212-867-5454, www.aburiyakinnosuke.com; hours: M–F 11:30AM–2:30PM, 5:30PM–12AM, Sa 5:30PM– 12AM, Su 5:30PM–11:30PM).* A unique and fun experience, diners have the option of grilling their own dishes right at their tables. The **Delegates' Dining Room (57) ($$)** *(UN, 4th floor, First Ave. at 46th St., 212-963-7626, www.aramark-un.com; reservations required for the public at least 24 hours in advance)* at the United Nations has the most eclectic clientele by far of any restaurant in the city, and offers amazing river views with its weekday-only lunch buffets. Men must wear jackets. Finally, Grand Central Terminal is home to the **Grand Central Oyster Bar (58) ($$)** *(see Grand Central Terminal on page 139, 212-490-6650, www.oysterbarny. com; hours: M–Sa 11:30AM–9:30PM)* in its lower level, where you can pig out on oysters and clam chowder in an elegant and truly iconic New York City space. The lower level food court offers everything from an Indian restaurant to cheesecake to go.

Bars & Nightlife:

The King Cole Bar at the St. Regis Hotel (59) *(2 E. 55th St., Fifth/Madison Aves., 212-339-6857, www.kingcole bar.com; hours: M–Sa 11:30AM–1AM, Su 12PM–12AM)* is *waaay* expensive, but the clubby armchairs, wooden paneling, and Maxfield Parrish mural behind the bar of King Cole himself make it worth every cent. The **Blue Bar at the Algonquin Hotel (60)** *(59 W. 44th St., Fifth/Sixth Aves., 212-840-6800, www.algonquin hotel.com/blue-bar; hours: daily 11:30AM–1AM)* is decorated with artwork of longtime Algonquin regular, Al Hirschfeld—featuring images from famous Broadway shows. The historic **P. J. Clarke's (61)** *(915 Third Ave at 55th St., 212-317-1616, www.pjclarkes. com; hours: daily kitchen 11:30AM–3AM, bar 11:30AM–4AM)* offers beer, music, and comfort food. *Mad Men* fans will recognize the interior. **The Campbell Apartment (62)** *(15 Vanderbilt Ave., 42nd/43rd Sts., 212-953-0409, www.hospitalityholdings.com; hours: M–Th 12PM–1AM, F–Sa 12PM–2AM, Su 12PM–12AM)* is a 1920s-era section of Grand Central Terminal, complete with 25-foot-high ceilings, that serves up jazz, cocktails, and a general Deco sensibility. **Turtle Bay Tavern (63)** *(987 2nd Ave., 52nd/53rd Sts., 212-223-4224, www.turtlebaynyc.com; hours: daily 12PM–4AM)* is a split-level taproom that's popular as an after-work hangout for the midtown work crew. Meet the after-five crowd at **Whiskey Blue (64)** *(541 Lexington Ave. at 49th St., 212-407-2947, www.gerber bars.com/whiskey-blue-ny; hours: M–Tu 4:30PM–2AM, W 4:30PM–3AM, Th 4PM–3AM, F 4PM–4AM, Sa 5PM–4AM, Su 5PM–2AM)*, part of the trendy W Hotel. Literati can head to **Bookmarks Rooftop Lounge and Terrace (81)** *(299 Madison Ave at 41st St., 212-204-5498, www.hospitality holdings.com; hours: Su–Th 4PM–12AM, F–Sa 4PM– 1AM)*, the rooftop bar at the boutique Library Hotel. It offers breathtaking cityscape views as well as charming literary-themed drinks, such as Tequila Mockingbird and The Pulitzer. For unabashed nostalgia lovers there's **The Monkey Bar (65)** *(60 E. 54th St., Madison/Park Aves., 212-288-1010, www.monkeybarnewyork.com; hours: M–F 11:30AM–1AM, Sa 5:30PM–1AM)*, a restaurant and bar that has a history dating back to Prohibition. In Murray Hill, **Artisanal (66)** *(2 Park Ave. at 32nd St., 212-725-8585; www.artisanalbistro.com, hours: lunch M–F 11:45AM–2:45PM, dinner M–W 5PM–9:45PM, Th–Sa 5PM–10:45PM, Su 5PM–8:45PM)* is a great bar and restaurant where cheese and wine rule. The folks here are serious about their tasting pleasures, and will help you find just the right fromage to go with that special glass of wine. If you're a foodie, this place is a must. **Les Halles (67)** *(411 Park Ave. South, E. 28th/E. 29th Sts., 212-679-4111, www.leshalles.net; hours: daily 7AM–12AM)*, celeb Chef Anthony Bourdain's former cooking ground, attracts a slick and well-heeled crowd for the brasserie food and extensive wine list. If you want a more casual experience here, simply sit at the bar with a drink and enjoy the excellent people-watching. **Joshua Tree (68)** *(513 Third Ave., E. 34th/E. 35th Sts., 212-689-0058, www.joshuatreebar.com; hours: M–F 11AM–4AM, Sa–Su 10AM–4AM)* is a good and friendly place to drop by for a beer or two, and the daily happy hour stretches from 12PM–8PM.

WHERE TO SHOP

A landmark since 1902, Saks Fifth Avenue (69) *(611 Fifth Ave. at 50th St., 212-753-4000, www.saks.com; hours: M–Sa 10AM–8PM, Su 11AM–7PM)* is one of the greatest of all New York's department stores. The men's and women's clothes, jewelry, perfumes, and gifts lean toward the pricey, but the service is not snobby. Just as smart is Bergdorf Goodman (70) *(754 Fifth Ave., 57th/58th Sts., 212-753-7300, www.bergdorf goodman.com; hours: M–Sa 10AM–8PM, Su 11AM–6PM),* where you'll see fur-coated ladies who lunch. Prices are steep, though the seasonal sales offer genuine bargains. Think you can't afford something at Tiffany & Co. (71) *(727 Fifth Ave, 56th/57th Sts., 212-755-8000, www. tiffany.com; hours: M–Sa 10AM–7PM, Su 12PM–6PM)?* Well, there are a few things the average purse can handle, including a silver bookmark (in that quintessential little blue box), and a few other items "under $175," as its website puts it. For high fashion there's Gucci (72) *(725 Fifth Ave., at 56th St., 212-826-2600, www. gucci.com; hours: M 10AM–7PM, Tu–W 10AM–6PM, Th–Sa 10AM–8PM, Su 12PM–7PM),* a place where you

will either feel entirely at home or run screaming through the door, depending on your tastes. At Chanel (73) *(15 E. 57th St., Fifth/Madison Aves., 212-355-5050, www.chanel.com; hours: M–W, F 10AM–6:30PM, Th*

10AM–7PM, Sa 10AM–6PM, Su 12PM–5PM) you can pick up a lipstick for a mere $20, or a suit for $2,000 and up. If you just want good, honest, no-nonsense men's clothes there's always Brooks Brothers (74) *(1270 Sixth Ave. at Rockefeller Center, 212-247-9374, www. brooksbrothers.com; hours: M–F 8AM–9PM, Sa 9AM–8PM; Su 10AM–7PM).* For literary types there's Bauman Rare Books (75) *(535 Madison Ave., 54th/55th Sts., 212-751-0011, www.baumanrarebooks.com; hours: M–Sa 10AM–6PM),* where first editions rule and you can ogle such beautiful bound editions as an original *Alice in Wonderland* or Darwin's *Origin of the Species.* For food, there's Grand Central Food Market (76) *(see Grand Central Terminal on page 139),* which has great delectables, particularly its meat, fish, and selection of fabulous cheese, as well as gift items such as chocolates and flowers. The lower level mall under Rockefeller Center (30) *(see Rockefeller Center on page 137)* features stores that sell everything from high-end chocolates to NYC key chains.

WHERE TO STAY

After a busy day of sight-seeing, rest your weary head on one of the variety of pillow styles available at the graceful and stylish **70 Park Avenue Hotel (77) ($$$$)** *(70 Park Ave., at 38th St., 212-973-2400, www.70parkave.com)*. This hotel is also pet-friendly so you don't have to leave Fido at home. **Hotel 31 (78) ($)** *(120 E. 31st St., Park Ave. S./Lexington Ave., 212-685-3060, www.hotel31.com)* is nowhere near as luxurious, but at around $79 a night and up, it's hard to complain. Money no object? You can't beat the **Waldorf Astoria Hotel (79) ($$$-$$$$)** *(301 Park Ave., at 50th St., 212-355-3000, waldorfnewyork. com)*—a Deco masterpiece where Frank Sinatra, Diana Ross, and a host of other well-known performers have entertained diners. The lobby's worth a look even if you aren't staying there. A much more reasonable (and hipper) option is the **Pod Hotel (80) ($$)** *(230 E. 51st St., Second/Third Aves., 212-355-0300, www.thepodhotel. com)*, with shared bathrooms for a number of rooms.

chapter 6

LINCOLN CENTER & ENVIRONS
UPPER WEST SIDE

LINCOLN CENTER & ENVIRONS UPPER WEST SIDE

Places to See:

1. Lincoln Center for the Performing Arts
1. Metropolitan Opera House
1. David H. Koch Theater
1. Walter Reade Theater
1. Film Society of Lincoln Center
2. Time Warner Center
3. Columbus Circle
4. Museum of Arts and Design
6. Merkin Concert Hall
7. Rose Theater
8. Dizzy's Club *Coca-Cola*
20. Ansonia Hotel
21. Central Park West
22. The Dakota
23. San Remo Apartments
24. Congregation Shearith Israel
25. Pomander Walk
26. Riverside Drive
27. Riverside Park
28. West 79th Street Marina and Boat Basin
29. American Museum of Natural History/ Rose Center for Earth and Space
30. Beacon Theatre
31. Symphony Space
32. El Taller Latino Americano
33. New-York Historical Society
34. Children's Museum of Manhattan

Places to Eat & Drink:

9. Per Se
10. Rosa Mexicano
11. Luce
12. Le Pain Quotidien
13. Stone Rose Lounge
14. The Rooftop
15. Cafe Fiorello
35. Island Burgers & Shakes
36. Josie's Restaurant
37. Cafe Blossom
38. Café Lalo
39. Alice's Tea Cup
40. Boat Basin Café
41. Café Luxembourg
42. Gray's Papaya
43. Bistro Citron
44. Carmine's
45. Flor De Mayo
46. Dive 75
47. Underground Lounge
48. Noi Due

LINCOLN CENTER & ENVIRONS

1 *to 66th St.-Lincoln Center;*
A C B D 1 *to 59th St.-Columbus Circle*

● SNAPSHOT ●

The neighborhood around the Lincoln Center for the Performing Arts was originally part of Hell's Kitchen, its neighbor to the south. The area was a vital, working-class neighborhood that sprawled westward to the Hudson and was infamous for its gangs and crime. Then in the early 1960s gentrification arrived in the newly minted form of "urban renewal," and the crumbling brownstones filled with lonely studios were converted back to family use again or demolished in great swaths to make way for—among other things—places such as Lincoln Center. The site is filled with venues, including the Metropolitan Opera House, David H. Koch Theater, and Avery Fisher Hall. Individually they're a fairly loveless group of buildings, but their saving grace is the wonderful main public plaza that unites them, and on a summer's night when the fountains are flowing there's no more magical spot to be in New York.

PLACES TO SEE
Landmarks:

Lincoln Center for the Performing Arts (1) *(W. 62nd to W. 66th Sts., Columbus/Amsterdam Aves., 212-875-5456 for event listings, www.lincolncenter.org)* is most impressive at night, when the buildings and fountain are all lit up. It's a fun spot to just hang out and watch New York's cease-less street parade. In the summer there's dancing in the plaza (see "Midsummer Night Swing" on its website). For individual attractions, see "Arts & Entertainment," page 155. The other major landmark here is the dynamic **Time Warner Center (2)** *(SW side of Columbus Circle, 58th/59th Sts., www.shopsatcolumbuscircle.com)*, a twin-towered glass monolith that rises far above everything else. Inside its shiny 2.8-million-square-foot, $1.7-billion interior, is a mini-city in itself, consisting of a hotel, condos, shops, restaurants, corporate headquar-ters, and more. *(See "Where to Shop," "Places to Eat & Drink," and "Arts & Entertainment.")* Everyone agreed that Columbus Circle needed a new building that would make a statement and help define this awkward circle-in-a-grid space, but its glossy opulence tends to polarize opinion: you'll either love it or hate it. Dwarfed

by this building is the statue of Columbus perched on his column in the center of **Columbus Circle (3)**, hand on hip as though in defiance at all that's going on around him. On the far side of Columbus Circle is the "lollipop building," originally designed as the **Gallery of Modern**

Art now the **Museum of Arts and Design (4)** *(2 Columbus Circle, Broadway/Eighth Ave., 212-299-7777, www.mad museum.org; hours: Tu–Su 10AM–6PM, Th–F 10AM–9PM)* showcasing crafts, arts, and design. You can't explore New York without encountering mega-developer Donald Trump's influence. Years ago he took over the old 44-story Gulf and Western building, had it re-clad at vast expense by architect Philip Johnson, and—voilà!—the **Trump International Hotel & Tower** *(1 Central Park West at Columbus Circle, 212-299-1000, www.trumpintl.com)* was born. The building is home to supermodels and baseball players, and anyone else who can afford the rent.

Arts & Entertainment:

Lincoln Center for the Performing Arts (1) *(see page 154)* is New York's altar of high culture, and whether it's ballet, opera, symphonic music, or film, you'll find it here at its finest. The **Metropolitan Opera House (1)** *(212-362-6000, www.metopera.org)* is the flashiest Lincoln Center building, located right in front of the plaza's main fountain, and offers a wide range of operas— from *Tosca* and *La Bohème*, that an opera novice will enjoy, to more esoteric fare. It has an excellent and informative website. The Met's own company is in residence September through May, and touring companies perform in the summer. The **David H. Koch Theater (1)** houses the **New York City Ballet** *(www.nycballet. com, 212-870-5505)*. The theater itself is magnificent, featuring inlaid Travertine marble floors, 40-foot gold leaf ceilings, dramatic spiral staircases and balconies overlooking the fountain in the Plaza of Lincoln Center. The **Walter Reade Theater (1)** *(212-875-5600, www. filmlinc.com, cash only at the box office)* is home to the **Film Society of Lincoln Center (1)**, which sponsors the annual New York Film Festival, as well as offering year-round viewings of films not otherwise available, plus revivals and directors' talks. A block away from all this highbrow activity is the excellent and quirky **Merkin Concert Hall (6)** *(Kaufman Center, 129 W. 67th St., Broadway/Amsterdam Ave., 212-501-3330, www. kaufman-center.org)*, which features jazz, experimental music, live broadcasts, and family theater matinees. The **Time Warner Center (2)** *(see page 154)* has several cultural hot spots, most notably the **Rose Theater (7)** *(Broadway at 60th St., 5th floor, 212-258-9800, www. jalc.org)*, a stunning glass-backed auditorium with amazing acoustics and sweeping views of Manhattan in the background. It hosts Lincoln Center's annual Jazz Festival, among other events. **Dizzy's Club** *Coca-Cola* **(8)** *(www.jalc.org)* is a more intimate retro-style jazz club, also on the fifth floor, that holds just 140 people. The **American Folk Art Museum** *(2 Lincoln Sq., Columbus Ave., at 66th St., 212-595-9533, www.folk artmuseum.org; hours: Tu–Th, F 12PM–7:30PM, Sa 11:30AM–7PM, Su 12PM–6PM)*, housing a delightful collection of early Americana, paintings, signboards, quilts, and temporary exhibitions.

PLACES TO EAT & DRINK
Where to Eat:

There's a cluster of restaurants and watering holes in the **Time Warner Center (2)** *(see page 154)*, including **Per Se (9) ($$$-$$$$)** *(4th floor, 212-823-9335, www.perse ny.com; hours: lunch F–Su 11:30AM–1:30PM, dinner M–Su 5:30PM–10PM)*, ace Chef Thomas Keller's fancy joint. Call months in advance if you want to score tables. Lincoln Center is, of course, surrounded by restaurants, and **Rosa Mexicano (10) ($$$)** *(61 Columbus Ave. at W. 62nd St., 212-977-7700, www.rosamexicano. com; hours: Su–M 11:30AM–10:30PM, Tu–Sa 11:30AM– 11:30PM)* offers fantastic Mexican food and great drinks. For delicious Italian with plenty of outdoor seating, try **Luce (11) ($$)** *(2014 Broadway, W. 67th/W. 68th Sts., 212-724-1400, www.lucenyc.com; hours: M–F 11:30AM–11PM, Sa 11AM–11:30PM, Su 11AM–11PM)*. If you need a quick, casual bite before catching a show at Lincoln Center, stop into **Le Pain Quotidien (12) ($)** *(60 W. 65th St. at Columbus Ave., 212-721-4001, www.lep ainquotidien.com; hours: daily 7AM–10PM)*. They have a variety of delicious baked goods, soups, salads, tartines, and more, to satisfy your taste buds.

Bars & Nightlife:

The **Time Warner Center (2)** *(see page 154)* offers a number of night life opportunities, the fanciest being Rande Gerber's **Stone Rose Lounge (13)** *(10 Columbus Circle, 4th floor, 212-823-9769, www. stoneroselounge.com; hours: M–W 3PM–2AM, Th–F 3PM–3AM, Sa 12PM–3AM, Su 12PM–12AM)*. The views of Central Park at night are pretty cool, and who knows—you may even bump into some celebrities. **The Rooftop (14)** *(44 W. 63rd St. at Broadway, 212-265-7400; www.empirehotelnyc.com; hours: Su–M 5PM–12AM, Tu–W 5PM–2AM, Th–Sa 5PM–4AM)*—the 12th floor bar at **The Empire Hotel (5)** *(see page 159)*—offers stellar views of Lincoln Center. Sit by the fireplace with a drink while gazing down on the glittering lights below. On warm-enough nights, take a seat at one of the sidewalk tables at **Cafe Fiorello (15)** *(1900 Broadway, 63rd/64th Sts., 212-595-5330, www.cafefiorello.com; hours: M–F 11:30AM–12:30AM, Sa 10AM–12:30AM, Su 10AM–11PM)* and, glass of wine in hand, watch the world saunter by.

WHERE TO SHOP

The **Time Warner Center (2)** *(see page 154)* has a collection of high-class stores, if money is no object, including **Swarovski**—for a crystal souvenir that will really sparkle. For lesser mortals there's always **J. Crew**, **Coach**, **Williams-Sonoma**, and the like. The **Whole Foods** supermarket here is the largest in New York, 59,000 square feet of impeccably displayed and carefully

chosen goods, along with a café and a sushi bar. Locals pack the place for quick pre-movie meals. Upstairs in the building lobby, cool gift shop **Mxyplyzyk** has a well-stocked kiosk. For household items there are two trusty stalwarts nearby, Pottery Barn (16) *(1965*

Broadway at W. 67th St., 212-579-8477, www.pottery barn.com; hours: M–Sa 10AM–9PM, Su 11AM–7PM) and Bed Bath & Beyond (17) *(1932 Broadway at W. 65th St., 917-441-9391, www.bedbathandbeyond.com; hours: daily 9AM–10PM).* There's also Gracious Home (18) *(1992 Broadway at 67th St., 212-231-7800, www.gracious home.com; hours: M–Sa 9AM–8:30PM, Su 10AM–7PM),* which, as its name implies, has hardware and house-wares to grace your home.

WHERE TO STAY

The area immediately around Lincoln Center is expen-sive, and you might want to consider moving a few blocks uptown to some of the Upper West Side's less expensive hotels *(see page 169)*. But if you do want to stay right by all the cultural action there's the **Mandarin Oriental New York (19)** *($$$$) (80 Columbus Circle at W. 60th St., 212-805-8800, www.mandarinoriental.com/ newyork),* part of the Time Warner complex; it offers amazing park views and prices to match. Or try **The Empire Hotel (5)** *($$$) (44 W. 63rd St. at Broadway, 212-265-7400; www.empirehotelnyc.com),* a sophisticated and sexy hotel that attracts an international crowd.

UPPER WEST SIDE

B C *to 72nd St., 81st St., 86th St., 96th St., 103rd St., Cathedral Parkway-110th St.;* **1** *to 79th St., 86th St., 96th St., 103rd St.;* **2 3** *to 72nd St., 96th St.*

● SNAPSHOT ●

The Upper West Side is the traditional liberal and intellectual heart of Manhattan, home to prominent museums and a wealthy, sophisticated populace. There's an endless and ongoing rivalry with the Upper East Side's denizens across the park, who are perceived by some to be more conservative, though the staggering escalation of real estate values and development on the West Side during the past few years has done much to blur this traditional boundary. It's *Seinfeld* territory, of course, and if Midtown is the iconic center of Manhattan with its skyscrapers, then the Upper West Side is the "regular guy" residential center of Manhattan for all those who aren't downtown-chic or Upper East Side-loaded: single or married with kids, this is where you come to live what passes for the "normal" life in Manhattan. The neighborhood is a great place to explore thanks to a vast array of restaurants, human-scaled side streets, and, of course, easy access to New York's great gem, Central Park, the development that brought the Upper West Side into being as a residential neighborhood in the first place during the late 19th century.

PLACES TO SEE
Landmarks:

The **Ansonia Hotel (20)** *(2109 Broadway, W. 73rd/W. 74th Sts., www.ansoniacondo.com)* is an amazing Beaux Arts building. But, despite the name, the Ansonia is an apartment building, not a hotel. Its developer was a stickler for quality construction, including sound-proof partitions, which resulted in numerous musicians living there, including Caruso and Stravinsky. Later it helped drown out the cries from Plato's Retreat, a notorious 1970s swinger club located there. **Central Park West (21)**, one of New York's most desirable addresses, runs up the west side of Central Park and is home to some of the finest residential build-ings in the city. **The Dakota (22)** *(1 W. 72nd St. at Central Park West)* is probably the most famous of them, former home to John Lennon and current home of his widow, Yoko Ono. Hard to imagine that, in 1884, it was one of the sole buildings in a remote neighborhood. If you look at Central Park West from Central Park, the Italian Renaissance-style twin towers of the **San Remo Apartments (23)** *(145-146 Central Park West, W. 74th/75th Sts.)* are among the most iconic. Bono bought a little pad in one of them for around $15 million, joining a nest of other celebs there—a tough thing to do,

considering Madonna was turned down by its co-op board. There are numerous religious and cultural institutions along Central Park West, and one of the handsomest is **Congregation Shearith Israel (24)** *(8 W. 70th St., www.shearith-israel. org)* a synagogue masquerading as a Georgian-style porticoed temple, built at the turn of the 19th century. The lovely brownstone residential blocks between the park and the Hudson River are well worth exploring. Pick a random route and you'll come across all sorts of unexpected architectural treats. One of the loveliest is **Pomander Walk (25)** *(W. 94th/W. 95th Sts., Broadway/West End Ave.),* an English-style mews of cottages running only one block and which creates a delightful mini-village atmosphere. **Riverside Drive (26)** *(W. 72nd St. to Fort Tryon Park)* is the other great residential address on the West Side, a majestic sweep that runs along the Hudson River and can best be appreciated from the water *(see Circle Line Cruises on page 118).* It's home to a combination of the old-moneyed intelligentsia and, increasingly, celebrities. Much of its charm derives from **Riverside Park (27)** *(W.*

72nd St. to W. 153rd St., www.river sideparkfund.org), which runs next to it along the river, and is a brilliantly landscaped creation of Frederick Law Olmsted, co-creator of Central Park. Make note to see the **West 79th Street Marina and Boat Basin**

(28) *(Hudson River at W. 79th St.)*, where a number of hardy souls, including entire families with children, live year-round on houseboats. There's also an excellent café there *(see* **Boat Basin Café (40)** *on page 165).*

Arts & Entertainment:

The most famous area museum is the **American Museum of Natural History (29)** *(main entrance Central Park West at W. 79th St., 212-769-5100, www.amnh.org; hours: daily 10AM–5:45PM)*, which stretches alongside Central Park between W. 77th and W. 81st Streets. There are endless models and skeletons of dinosaurs, reptiles, and fish, as well as changing exhibits, an IMAX theater, and count- less buttons to push. The museum is also home to the **Rose Center for Earth and Space (29)**, a planetarium in an astounding glass box that will whisk you away on virtual reality tours to

Mars and beyond. It's not to be missed. If you love live music, the Upper West Side is home to the **Beacon Theatre (30)** *(2124 Broadway, W. 74th/W. 75th Sts., 212-465-6500, www.beacontheatre.com)* a mid-sized venue originally built in 1928 as a vaudeville palace that plays host to both lesser-known acts and, when they're looking for a more intimate setting, huge acts like Ringo Starr and Bob Dylan. **Symphony Space (31)** *(2537 Broadway at W. 95th St., 212-864-5400, www.symphonyspace.org)* offers offbeat performance art of all kinds, including excellent dance, literature, and film series, plus family theater events. At **El Taller Latino Americano (32)** *("The Latin American Workshop")*

(2710 Broadway at W. 104th St., 212-665-9460, www. tallerlatino.org) you'll find classes and workshops from flamenco dancing to guitar playing, as well as frequent visits by Latino arts organizations. The **New-York Historical Society (33)** *(170 Central Park West at 77th St., 212-873-3400, www.nyhistory.org; hours: Tu–Th, Sa 10AM–6PM, F 10AM–8PM, Su 11AM–5PM)* is a treasure trove of reading material and historical collections, including John James Audubon watercolors.

Kids:

The **Children's Museum of Manhattan (34)** *(212 W. 83rd St., Broadway/Amsterdam Ave., 212-721-1223, www. cmom.org; hours: Tu–Su 10AM–5PM, Sa 10AM–7PM)* is a terrific resource for kids, offering play areas, drawing and music classes, workshops, interactive exhibits, and more. The casual **Island Burgers & Shakes (35)** *($)* *(422 Amsterdam Ave. at 80th St., 212-877-7943, hours: Su–Th 12PM-10PM, F–Sa 12PM-11PM)* has a myriad of burgers and sandwiches to choose from that kids will love.

PLACES TO EAT & DRINK
Where to Eat:

Get your organic fix at **Josie's Restaurant (36)** *($$)* *(300 Amsterdam Ave., at 74th St., 212-769-1212, www.josies nyc.com; hours: M–F 12PM–10PM, Sa 10AM–11PM, Su 10AM–10PM)*, where you'll find healthful, wholesome, (and yes, delicious!) food. Even non-vegans will be tempted by the diverse and creative menu at **Cafe Blossom (37)** *($$)* *(466 Columbus Ave., 82nd/83rd Sts., 212-875-2600, www.blossomnyc.com; hours: M–F 11:30AM–10PM, Sa 11AM–11:30PM, Su 11AM–10PM)*. The soy bacon cheeseburger with caramelized onions and chipotle aioli is divine. **Café Lalo (38) ($-$$)** *(201 W. 83rd St., Amsterdam Ave./Broadway, 212-496-6031, www.cafelalo.com; hours: M–Th 8AM–2AM, F 8AM–4AM, Sa*

9AM–4AM, Su 9AM–2AM) is brightly lit and crowded, but good for coffee and desserts. **Alice's Tea Cup (39) ($-$$)** *(102 W. 73rd St., Amsterdam/Columbus Aves., 212-799-3006, www.alicesteacup.com; hours: daily 8AM–8PM)* has a cozy atmosphere, 200 blends of tea, and fairy wings kids can borrow while enjoying their meals. The **Boat Basin Café (40) ($$-$$$$)** *(W. 79th St. at the Hudson River, 212-496-5542, www.boatbasincafe.com; hours: open late Mar–Oct M–W 12PM–11PM, Th–F 12PM–11:30PM, Sa 11AM–11:30PM, Su 11AM–10PM)* has great views and some of the best and most friendly barbecues in the city. **Café Luxembourg (41) ($$$)** *(200 W. 70th St., Amsterdam/Columbus Aves., 212-873-7411, www.cafeluxembourg. com; hours: M–Tu 8AM–11PM, W–F 8AM–12AM, Sa 9AM–12AM, Su 9AM–11PM)* is a neighborhood classic. Great bistro food, very styl-

ish, and always crowded. Love hot dogs and a bargain? **Gray's Papaya (42) ($)** *(2090 Broadway at W. 72nd St., 212-799-0243; hours: daily 24 hours)* can't be beat for its delicious dogs and cool fruit drinks. Heading uptown a bit, **Bistro Citron (43) ($-$$)** *(473 Columbus Ave., W. 82nd/W. 83rd Sts., 212-400-9401, www.bistrocitronnyc. com; hours: lunch M–Sa 12PM–3PM; dinner Su–Th 5PM–*

10PM, F–Sa 5PM–11PM; brunch Sa–Su 11AM–3PM) offers French comfort foods. Long-time favorite **Carmine's (44) ($$)** *(2450 Broadway, W. 90th/W. 91st Sts., 212-362-2200, www.carminesnyc. com; hours: Su–Th 11:30AM–11PM, F–Sa 11:30AM–12AM)* is for really pigging out on huge portions of basic Italian; best for groups and family outings. For a new kind of fusion, **Flor De Mayo (45) ($$)** *(2651 Broadway at 101st St., 212-663-5520, www.flordemayo.com; hours: daily 12PM–12AM)* serves up Chinese-Peruvian cuisine. They also specialize in the perfect roast chicken. Excellent food, good service, and prices that won't break the bank—who could ask for more?

Bars & Nightlife:

Dive 75 (46) *(101 W. 75th St. at Columbus Ave., 212-362-7518;*  *www.divebarnyc.com; hours: M– Th 5PM–4AM, F 3PM–4AM, Sa– Su 12PM–4AM)* is a friendly spot that stocks great beers and lots of board games. The **Underground Lounge (47)** *(955 West End Ave., at 107th St., 212-531-4759, www. theundergroundnyc.com; hours: M–Th 4PM–2AM, F–Sa 4PM–4AM, Su 12PM–4AM)* hosts comedy shows, live music, and open mic nights. **Noi Due (48)** *(143 W. 69th St., Broadway/Columbus Ave., 212-712-2222, www.noiduecafe.com; hours: M–Th 11AM–11PM, Sa* *after sundown–1AM, Su 11AM–10:30PM)* serves delicious traditional Italian cuisine with a slight twist: it's all kosher. Choose from an extensive list of pizzas, with over 20 kosher wines to pair with them. The decor is simple yet cozy, making this both a lovely date spot as well as a comfortable

place to just enjoy great food. Founded by soul duo Ashford & Simpson, **Sugar Bar (49)** *(254 W. 72nd St., Broadway/West End Ave., 212-579-0222, www.sugarbarnyc.com; hours: Tu–W 5PM–11PM, Th–Sa 5PM–1AM)* has live soul and jazz and a reasonable cover. It also does a gospel brunch on Sundays. The drinks and food are good—very good—but the jazz, oh that jazz, is the real draw at **Smoke Jazz & Supper Club (50)** *(2751 Broadway at 106th St., 212-864-6662; www.smokejazz.com; hours: M–Sa 5:30PM–3AM, Su 11AM–3AM)*. Big names show up to play here. The **Abbey Pub (51)** *(237 W. 105th, near corner of Broadway, 212-*

222-8713; hours: M–Sa 4PM–4AM, Su 12PM–4AM) is the place for you if you take your drinking seriously. Beers, burgers, and three TV screens for watching sports make it a favorite local spot. Beware the more exotic fare on the menu.

WHERE TO SHOP

You can't say you've been to the Upper West Side till you've been to **Zabar's (52)** *(2245 Broadway at W. 80th St., 212-787-2000, www.zabars.com; hours: M–F 8AM–7:30PM, Sa 8AM–8PM, Su 9AM–6PM)*, a food-cum-household appliance store that has amazing prices and great quality. The

place is packed on the weekends. **Harry's Shoes (53)** *(2299 Broadway at W. 83rd St., 855-642-7797, www.harrys-shoes.com; hours: Tu–W, F–Sa 10AM–6:45PM, M, Th 10AM–7:45PM, Su 11AM–6PM)* has catered to generations of New Yorkers since its opening in 1931. Comfort footwear and knowledgeable salespeople are its specialties. They also have a kids store located down the block. For a trifecta of food shopping classics, check out **Barney Greengrass (54)** *(541 Amsterdam Ave., W. 86th/W. 87th Sts., 212-724-4707, www.barneygreengrass.com; hours: Tu–Su 8AM–6PM)* with its pricey but fabulous sturgeon, lox, bialys, and more. For clothes try **Barneys Co-Op (55)** *(2151 Broadway at W. 75th St., 646-335-0978, www.barneys.com; hours: M–F 10AM–8PM, Sa 10AM–7PM, Su 11AM–7PM)*, a hipper, edgier spinoff of the main Barneys store on Madison Avenue *(see page 182)*. For

romantic, feminine, one-of-a-kind skirts, dresses, and more, stop into **Älskling (56)** *(228 Columbus Ave., W. 70th/W. 71st Sts., 917-558-1167, www.tvillingonline.com; hours: M–Sa*

11AM–7PM, Su 1PM–5PM). The boutique's name means "darling" in Swedish. Robert Marc (57) *(190 Columbus Ave., W. 68th/W. 69th Sts., 212-799-4600, www.robert marc.com; hours: M–F 10AM–7PM, Sa 10AM–6PM, Su 12PM–6PM)* has several stores around town offering some seriously cool spectacles. Finally, if you like the thrill of the hunt, check out the GreenFlea (58) *(Columbus Ave., 76th/77th Sts., 212-239-3025, www.greenfleamarkets.com; hours: Nov–Mar Sa–Su 10AM–5:30PM, Apr–Oct Sa–Su 10AM–6PM).* You can not only find amazing vintage and handcrafted items, but proceeds benefit several of the neighborhood's public schools.

WHERE TO STAY

The Hotel Belleclaire (59) **($$)** *(250 W. 77th St. at Broadway, 212-362-7700, www.hotelbelleclaire.com)* offers 230 rooms in a stunning early 20th-century building. On the Ave Hotel (60) **($$)** *(2178 Broadway at W. 77th St., 212-362-1100, www.ontheave-nyc.com)* is a mid-priced hotel with great views of Central Park and more style than many hotels in this neighborhood.

chapter 7

UPPER EAST SIDE

CENTRAL PARK

UPPER EAST SIDE CENTRAL PARK

Places to See:

1. 11 East 62nd Street
2. 11 East 73rd Street
3. 45 East 66th Street Apartments
4. Carl Schurz Park
5. Gracie Mansion
6. Jewish Museum
7. Solomon R. Guggenheim Museum
8. Cooper-Hewitt National Design Museum
9. Rhinelander Mansion
10. METROPOLITAN MUSEUM OF ART ★
11. National Academy Museum
12. Neue Galerie
13. Museum of American Illustration
14. Frick Collection
15. Asia Society and Museum
45. The Pond
46. Wollman (Trump) Rink
47. The Dairy
48. Central Park Zoo
49. Heckscher Playground
50. Sheep Meadow
51. Strawberry Fields
52. The Lake
53. Loeb Boathouse
54. Bow Bridge
55. Bethesda Fountain and Terrace
56. The Ramble
57. Delacorte Theater
58. Belvedere Castle/ Henry Luce Nature Observatory
59. The Great Lawn
60. Jacqueline Kennedy Onassis Reservoir
61. North Meadow Recreation Center
62. Harlem Meer
63. Conservatory Garden
64. Charles A. Dana Discovery Center
65. The Carousel
66. Tisch Children's Zoo

★ Top Picks

Places to Eat & Drink:

Where to Shop:

Where to Stay:

UPPER EAST SIDE

4 5 *to 59th St. or 86th St.;* **6** *to 59th St., 68th St.,*
77th St., 86th St., 96th St., 103rd St., 110th St.;
N R Q *to Fifth Ave.-59th St., Lexington Ave.-59th St.*

● **SNAPSHOT** ●

The Upper East Side is an astonishingly varied and rich
(in every sense of the word) part of the city. A brief stroll
around the ritzier stretches of Fifth or Madison Avenues
will certainly reveal more than a fair share of frosty
blondes with Pekingese in tow or imperious old ladies
being helped out of taxis by their doormen, but it's
much more than that. The stretches east of Lexington
Avenue resemble the Upper West Side in their relatively
democratic social makeup. There is also the cultural
bounty of the area to consider: "Museum Mile" with its
amazing cluster of world-class museums, and some of
the most beautiful architecture in the city.

PLACES TO SEE
Landmarks:

The heart of chic and moneyed New
York is the so-called **"Gold Coast,"**
which runs for about a mile
between E. 60th and E. 80th
Streets from Fifth Avenue to
Park Avenue. This was the area
where the gilded-age robber bar-
ons built their mansions along

Central Park. Many of these buildings have since been converted either to apartments or consulates. One of the most amazing is **11 E. 62nd Street (1)** *(Fifth/Madison Aves.)*, a former private mansion now home to Japan's UN representative. The opulence of its limestone facade and Beaux Arts details still amazes today in a world of Donald Trump high-rises. Another example is **11 E. 73rd St. (2)** *(Fifth/Madison Aves.)*, originally the Joseph and Kate Pulitzer House (of Pulitzer Prize renown), now converted into apartments. Around the turn of the 19th century the rich began to leave their beautiful, yet hard-to-keep-up, mansions and moved to the latest architectural invention—the apartment building. Naturally they sacrificed nothing in terms of style, as the **45 East 66th Street Apartments (3)** *(Madison/Park Aves.)* demonstrate. With its lovely Gothic details and large windows it's as desirable a residence today as it was nearly 100 years ago. With an average per-resident income of around $200,000 a year (south of E. 96th Street, that is), Park Avenue deserves its wealthy reputation. The avenue was built over railroad tracks that had been an open trench and eyesore for many years. They were covered over around the turn of the century. At E. 96th Street, Park Avenue's little secret emerges from underground and the character of the street and the surrounding neighborhood changes drastically. It's fun to watch the trains come crawling out of the dark here. Along the waterfront there's **Carl Schurz Park (4)** *(East River between E. 84th/E. 90th Sts., www.carlschurzparknyc.org)*, a beautifully designed park built out ingeniously over the FDR Drive below. It affords amazing views across to Queens on the other side. The park contains the Mayor's official residence, **Gracie Mansion (5)** *(E. 88th St. at East End Ave., 212-570-4773. Call for updated tour information)*. Gracie Mansion is Manhattan's sole remaining Federal-style house.

The designation "Upper East Side" incorporates several residential areas that are worth exploring, including **Carnegie Hill** *(E. 86th to E. 96th Sts., Fifth/Third Aves.)* and **Yorkville** *(E. 72nd to E. 96th Sts., Central Park/East River)*. Both are filled with elegant tree-lined streets and fine shops and restaurants. Carnegie Hill in particular is home to a number of superb museums, including the **Jewish Museum (6)** *(1109 Fifth Ave. at E. 92nd St., 212-423-3200, www.thejewishmuseum.org: Sa–Tu 11AM–5:45PM, Th 11AM–8PM, F 11AM–4PM, closed W)*; the **Solomon R. Guggenheim Museum (7)** *(1071 Fifth Ave. at E. 89th St., 212-423-3500, www.guggenheim.org; hours: Su–W, F 10AM–5:45PM, Sa 10AM–7:45PM)*; and the **Cooper-Hewitt National Design Museum (8)** *(2 E. 91st St. at Fifth Ave., 212-849-8400, www.cooper hewitt.org; M–F, Sa 10AM–9PM, Su 10AM–6PM)*, which was converted from steel magnate Andrew Carnegie's private 1902 mansion. Yorkville became a notably German neighborhood, and the wealthy Rhinelander family in particular built many beautiful mansions and apartment buildings here in conjunction with architect Henry Hardenbergh, designer of the Dakota building. The most famous of these is the **Rhinelander Mansion (9)** *(867 Madison Ave., E. 71st/E. 72nd Sts.)*, a stunning building, both inside and out, that's now home to Ralph Lauren's Polo empire in New York.

Arts & Entertainment:

The Upper East Side is high-brow heaven, with the greatest concentration of museums in the city. **"Museum Mile"** is the name given to the stretch of cultural institutions that runs along Fifth Avenue from E. 82nd to E. 104th Streets. The biggest and most famous of them all is the ★**METROPOLITAN MUSEUM OF ART (10)** *(1000 Fifth Ave. at E. 82nd St., 212-535-7710, www. metmuseum.org; hours: Su–Th 10AM–5:30PM, F–Sa 10AM–9PM)*, a vast treasure house that runs four blocks north up Fifth Avenue and into Central Park at the back. The Met's slogan is "5,000 years of art," and they aren't kidding; walking into its vast central rotunda with galleries radiating off it can be intimidating. The permanent collection offers something for everyone, from paintings to photographs to musical instruments to textiles. Each month brings special exhibitions. It's best to choose a particular part—European painting, Egyptian art—and enjoy it in detail rather than attempt to try to see it all. On Fridays and Saturdays the Met hosts a string quartet and cocktails upstairs. The recently-renovated American Wing Galleries include a sculpture garden that invites lingering. From classical temple to outrageous modern swirl, the Frank Lloyd Wright-designed Solomon R. Guggenheim Museum (7) *(1071 Fifth Ave. at E. 89th St., 212-423-3500, www.guggen*

TOP PICK!

heim.org; hours: Su–W, F, 10AM–5:45PM, Sa 10AM–7:45PM) seems to twist itself out of the ground. Inside, this spiral is even more amazing, though opinion is divided about how success- ful a space it is to actually view the modern art on exhibit there. Farther north  is the **Cooper-Hewitt National Design Museum (8)** *(2 E. 91st St. at Fifth Ave., 212-849-8400, www.cooperhewitt. org; M–F, Su 10AM–6PM, Sa 10AM–9PM)*, a handsome limestone-clad building dedicated to the history of design. Expect to find exhibitions covering eclectic subject matter from wallpaper to silverware to classic 1960s road maps, to name a few recent ones. The **Jewish Museum (6)** *(1109 Fifth Ave. at E. 92nd St., 212-423-3200, www.thejewishmuseum.org: Su–Tu, Sa 11AM–5:30PM, 8PM on Th, F 11AM–4PM, closed W)* is housed in a 1908 chateau and has a large permanent collection of artifacts related to Jewish life and culture, in addition to hosting impressive temporary exhibi- tions. There's also a kosher café. The **National Academy Museum (11)** *(1083 5th Ave., at 89th St., 212-369-4880, www.nationalacademy.org, hours: W–Su 11AM–6PM)* promotes American art through exhibitions and houses one of the largest public collections of 19th- and 20th-century art in the U.S. The **Neue Galerie (12)** *(1048 5th Ave., at 86th St., 212-628-6200, www.neue galerie.org; hours: Th–M 11AM–6PM)*, housed in an historical landmark building designed by Carrère &

Hastings, displays early 20th-century German and Austrian art and design pieces. After perusing the galleries, enjoy a snack—the sausage and soft pretzel plate is divine—at one of the museum's two cafés. Sit upstairs if there's no line, head downstairs to Café Fledermaus if there's a wait. Off Museum Mile are a few other interesting museums, including the **Museum of American Illustration (13)** *(128 E. 63rd St., Park/Lexington Aves., 212-838-2560, www.societyillustrators.org; hours: Tu 10AM–8PM, W–F 10AM–5PM, Sa 12PM–4PM)*. Located in the Society of Illustrators, this museum offers a stunning collection of hundreds of works by many of the greatest names in American painting and illustration. Far more sedate is the **Frick Collection (14)** *(1 E. 70th St., Fifth/Madison Aves., 212-288-0700, www.frick.org; hours: Tu–Sa 10AM–6PM, Su 11AM–5PM)*, a charming classical mansion once owned by industrialist Henry Clay Frick. It has a garden surrounding it, an indoor pond, and a terrific collection of old masters, including Vermeer, van Dyke, and Rembrandt. Finally, there's the **Asia Society and Museum (15)** *(725 Park Ave. at E. 70th St., 212-288-6400, www.asiasociety.org; hours: Tu–Su 11AM–6PM)*, housed in a sleek modern building with a

 spacious interior that does justice to the delicacy of the works on display. There's an Asian restaurant attached where the food is artfully prepared and just as pleasing to the taste buds.

Kids:

Carl Schurz Park (4) *(East River between E. 84th/E. 90th Sts.)* is wonderful for children, in particular the playground at E. 84th Street and East End Avenue. **EJ's Luncheonette**  **(16)** *(1271 Third Ave. at E. 73rd St., 212-472-0600, www. ejsluncheonette.com: M–Sa 7:30AM–11PM, Su 7:30AM–10:30PM)* is loud, kid-friendly, and cheap. Reward good-at-the-museums behavior (and yourself) with divine baked goods at **Two Little Red Hens (17) ($)** *(1652 Second Ave. at 86th St., 212-452-0476; www.twolittleredhens. com; hours: M–Th 7:30AM–9PM, F 7:30AM–10PM, Sa 8AM–10PM, Su 8AM–8PM)*.

PLACES TO EAT & DRINK
Where to Eat:

The Upper East Side rarely gets the attention it deserves for its restaurants, although everybody knows **Serendipity3 (18) ($$)** *(225 E. 60th St., 2nd/3rd Aves., 212-838-3531, www.serendipity3.com; hours: Su–Th 11:30AM–12AM, F–Sa 11:30AM–1AM)*. It holds a Guinness World Record for the most expensive sundae—coming in at $1,000—it's covered in edible gold leaf. But what people really come here for is the famous "Frrrozen Hot Chocolate." Little known fact: they make a mean burger. Be prepared to wait for a table. **Daniel (19) ($$$$)** *(60 E. 65th St., Madison/Park Aves., 212-288-0033, www.danielnyc.com; hours: M–Sa 5:30PM–11PM)* is an institution for contemporary French cuisine, owned by well-known Chef Daniel Boulud. For good burgers and other American fare there's **Jackson Hole (20) ($$)** *(232 E. 64th St., Second/Third Aves., 212-371-7187, www.jacksonholeburgers.com; hours: M–Th 10:30AM–1AM, F–Sa 10:30AM–1:30AM, Su 10:30AM–12AM).* In the 70s there's **Due (21) ($$)** *(1396 Third Ave., E. 79th/E. 80th Sts., 212-772-3331, www.duenyc.com; hours: Su–Th 12PM–12AM, F–Sa 12PM–1AM)* for good Northern Italian. The all-vegan menu at **Candle Café (22) ($$)** *(1307 Third Ave., 74th/75th Sts., 212-472-0970; www.candlecafe.com; M–Sa 11:30AM–10:30PM, Su 11:30AM–9:30PM)* pulls in crowds of every dietary persuasion. In the 80s there's **Beyoglu (23) ($$)** *(1431 Third Ave. at E. 81st St., 212-650-0850; hours: daily 12PM–10:30PM),* an excellent Mediterranean-Turkish place where the best thing to do is share a bunch of the fresh appetizers. During warm weather, it's especially nice to feast on Italian cuisine at the outdoor garden seating available at **Vespa (24) ($$)** *(1625 Second Ave., E. 84th/85th Sts., 212-472-2050, www.vespauno.com; hours: M–F 5PM–11PM, Sa–Su 12PM–3PM, 4:30PM–11PM).* A remnant of the old German community in Yorkville is **Heidelberg (25) ($$)** *(1648 Second Ave., E. 85th/E. 86th Sts., 212-628-2332, www.heidelberg-nyc.com; hours: daily 11:30AM–11PM),* which has kitschy decor but solid portions. The delicious food as well as the inviting atmosphere makes the French restaurant **Café d'Alsace (68) ($$)** *(1695 Second Ave., E. 88th Sts., 212-722-5133, hours: M–W 10:30AM–11PM, Th–F 10:30AM–12AM, Sa 9AM–12AM, Su 9AM–11PM)* a Yorkville go-to for brunch. Try the Omelette d'Alsace with a Bowl of Café Au Lait. In the 90s, try **Vico (26) ($$$)** *(1302 Madison Ave., E. 92nd/E. 93rd Sts., 212-876-2222, cash only; hours daily 12PM–3PM, 5PM–11PM)* if you want to splurge on really good Italian food. An unusual Brazilian outpost up here is **Zebú Grill (27) ($$)** *(305 E. 92nd St., First/Second Aves., 212-426-7500, www.zebugrill.com; hours: M–Tu 5PM–11PM, W–F 5PM–11:30PM, Sa 12PM–11:30PM, Su 12PM–11PM)*, which offers a really lively vibe, and truly flavorful food.

Bars & Nightlife:

Stir (28) *(1363 First Ave. at E. 73rd St., 212-744-7190, www.stirnyc.com; hours: Tu–W 5PM–1AM, Th 5PM–2AM, F 5PM–3AM, Sa 5PM–4AM)* is an exposed-brick minimalist bar with a sceney downtown feel—and a wide variety of speciality cocktails. Far more old-school is **Harry Cipriani (29)** *(781 Fifth Ave., E. 59th/E. 60th Sts., 212-753-5566, www.cipriani.com; hours: daily 7AM–12AM)*, where waiters in tuxes create a potentially daunting atmosphere for some, though it's a true New York experience. **Club Macanudo (30)** *(26 E. 63rd St., Park/Madison Aves., 212-752-8200, www.clubmacanudo.com; hours: M–Tu 12PM–1AM, W–Sa 12PM–2AM, Su 12PM–10PM)* is for those who like to smoke cigars while swilling a single malt. (Yes! You can still smoke here.) It's pricey and you need to dress up. **Bemelmans Bar (31)** *(Carlyle Hotel, 35 E. 76th St. at Madison Ave., 212-744-1600, www.the carlyle.com; daily 12PM–12:30AM)* is classic New York—a gentleman's club ambience with plush chairs, cozy decor, steep drinks, and wonderful live jazz. If all this is a bit too mature for your taste, there's another, more youthful, aspect to the Upper East Side's bar and club scene, as represented by **Kinsale Tavern (32)** *(1672 Third Ave., at E. 93rd St., 212-348-4370, www.kinsale.com; hours: M–F 12PM–4AM,*

Sa–Su 8AM–4AM), a rowdy Irish pub that boasts 30 beers on tap and many screens to take in U.S. and international sports games. A more hipster, trendy choice would be **The Penrose (69)** *(1590 Second Ave., E. 82nd/E. 83rd Sts., 212-203-2751, hours: M–Th 3PM–4AM, F 12PM–4AM, Sa–Su 10:30AM–4AM)*. The favorite spot for Yorkville young professionals, The Penrose has a classy '30s vibe with a delectable list of cocktails and craft beers. If wine is more your style, try **Vero Uptown (33)** *(1483 Second Ave., 77th/78th Sts., 212-452-3354; www.vero-nyc.com; hours: M–W 4PM–12AM, Th–F 4PM–1AM, Sa 2PM–1AM, Su 2PM–11PM)*, a wine bar that also serves tasty paninis.

WHERE TO SHOP

The Upper East Side's prime shopping strip is Madison Avenue, where all the famous designers have their flagship stores. Parisian-style merchant **Hermès (34)** *(691 Madison Ave. at E. 62nd St., 212-751-3181, www.hermes.com; hours: M–W 10AM–6PM, Th 10AM–7PM, F–Sa 10AM–6PM)* offers its famous scarves and much more at this spacious store. If you're willing to invest in shoes, then **Jimmy Choo (35)** *(716 Madison Ave., E. 63rd/E. 64th Sts., 212-759-7078, www.jimmychoo.com; hours: M–W, F–Sa 10AM–6PM, Th 10AM–7PM, Su 12PM–6PM)* is your nirvana. You can find sexy high-heeled creations that will make you feel part of the *Sex and the City* cast. **Barneys New York (36)** *(660 Madison Ave. at E. 61st St., 212-826-8900, www.barneys.com; hours: M–F 10AM–8PM, Sa 10AM–7PM, Su 11AM–6PM)* has classic menswear and women's clothes too, as well as a beauty store, a super-cool restaurant, and price tags that might startle budget shoppers. **Prada (37)** *(841 Madison Ave.*

at E. 70th St., 212-327-4200, www.prada.com; hours: M–W, F–Sa 10AM–6PM, Th 10AM–7PM, Su 12PM–5PM) sells a whole range of men and women's wear, but it's those shoes with the little red tag on the heel that really count. **Morgane Le Fay (38)** *(980 Madison Ave., E. 76th/E. 77th Sts., 212-879-9700, www.morganelefay.com; hours: M–Sa 10AM–6PM, Su 12PM–5PM)* offers beautifully bizarre, almost architectural gowns and dresses at  suitably architectural prices. Less expensive stores can be found east of Lexington Avenue. Ratcheting down the prices considerably is the **Memorial Sloan-Kettering Cancer Center Thrift Shop (39)** *(1440 Third Ave., E. 81st/E. 82nd Sts., 212-535-1250; hours: M–Sa 10:30AM–6PM, Su 11:30AM–5PM)*, which has some real bargains, as the ladies who lunch often drop off their unwanted couture here. This is one of the best thrift shops in the city. At **Pookie & Sebastian (40)** *(1488 Second Ave., E. 77th/E. 78th Sts., 212-861-0550; hours: M–W 11AM–8PM, Th–Sa 11AM–9PM, Su 11AM–7PM)* you can get cutting-edge fashion, including a whole array of designer jeans, at much reduced prices. If you're a hi-fi nut, **Lyric Hi Fi, Inc. (41)** *(1221 Lexington Ave., E. 82nd/E. 83rd Sts., 212-439-1900, www.lyricusa.com; hours: M–Sa 10AM–6PM)* is an audiophile's playground. Finally, 86th Street is like a mall without a roof. Dozens of familiar brands line the streets.

WHERE TO STAY

If money's no object you can't beat the venerable **Carlyle Hotel (42) ($$$$)** *(35 E. 76th St., Madison/Park Aves., 212-744-1600, www.thecarlyle.com)*. It is home to **Bemelmans Bar (31)** *(see page 181)*, famous for its animal murals by Ludwig Bemelmans, the creator of the *Madeline* books, who was a former resident of the hotel. There's live music with a steep cover, but it's worth it. The 100-year-old **Hotel Wales (43) ($$-$$$)** *(1295 Madison Ave. at E. 92nd St., 212-876-6000, www.hotelwalesnyc.com)* is a lovely hotel that feels like you're entering a private (albeit grand) house. It's also very pet- and child-friendly. There is also the **Gracie Inn (44) ($$-$$$)** *(502 E. 81st. St., York/East End Aves., 212-628-1700, www.gracieinn hotel.com)*, tucked away in a town house far from the subway, but close to a local bus stop and all the taxis you could ever hope to hail.

CENTRAL PARK

To East Side of the Park:
4 5 *to 59th St. or 86th St.;* **6** *to 59th St., 68th St., 77th St., 86th St., 96th St., 103rd St., 110th St.*

To West Side of the Park:
B C *to 59th St.-Columbus Circle, 72nd St., 81st St., 86th St., 96th St., 103rd St., 110th St.-Cathedral Parkway;* **A** *to 59th St.-Columbus Circle*

To Southern Side of the Park:
B D E *to Seventh Ave.;*
N Q R *to 57th St.-Seventh Ave.;*
F *to 57th St.;* **N R Q** *to Fifth Ave.-59th St.*

To Northern Side of the Park:
2 3 *to Central Park North-110th St.*

● SNAPSHOT ●

It's impossible to conceive of New York without ★**CENTRAL PARK**, yet for years the city existed without any major public park for its teeming populace. Old photographs and engravings reveal a rocky expanse com-

plete with wooden shacks, grazing goats, swamps, and encampments of the city's dispossessed. In the mid-19th century, the city's elders were finally piqued by their great rivals in London and Paris to do something about this, and commissioned landscape designer Frederick Law Olmsted and architect Calvert Vaux to convert a vast chunk of this unruly land into a picturesque European-style park worthy of a great city. This of course they did (along with several other parks in New York), and the results were astonishing. Not only did New York gain an enormous and beautiful green space, but the effect was also to galvanize development around the park, turning what even in the 1880s was still a largely undeveloped rural suburb of the city into a social and architectural center every bit the equal of its European counterparts.

PLACES TO SEE
Landmarks:
Southern Section (Central Park South to 72nd Street):

Olmsted and Vaux adopted the three principal elements of 18th-century British Picturesque design—water, landscaping, and architecture—to create their masterpiece, and these elements have only improved with time. Enter Central Park from the southeast and you'll encounter **The Pond (45)** *(approx. Fifth/Sixth Aves. between 60th/62nd Sts.)*—an artfully placed body of water with ducks and swans floating on it. Turn around and gaze south over The Pond at the skyline of Central

Park South rising above it for one of the most knockout views in the city. Just north of The Pond is the outdoor **Wollman (Trump) Rink (46)** *(just north of the park entrance at Sixth Ave./Central Park South, www.wollmanskatingrink.com:*

In Season: M–Tu 10AM–2:30PM, W–Th 10AM–10PM, F–Sa 10AM–11PM, Su 10AM–9PM)—which, like the Rink at Rockefeller Center, offers equal chances of romance and public embarrassment. Built in the 1950s, it fell into disrepair, with the city unable to restore it. Enter Donald Trump on a white horse. He not only repaired the rink ahead of schedule, but did so $750,000 under budget. Naturally, it's now emblazoned with his name. Just north of the rink is **The Dairy (47)** *(mid-park at 65th St.)*, Vaux's delightful Victorian Gothic confection. It used to be a real working dairy, but now operates as an information center for the park, and the official gift store *(212-794-6564 for details)*. The other major landmarks in this southern section of the park are the **Central Park Zoo (48)** *(830 Fifth Ave., E. 63rd/E. 66th Sts., 212-439-6500, www.central parkzoo.org; hours: Nov–March 10AM–4:30PM, April–Oct 10AM–5PM, weekends and holidays 10AM–5:30PM)* and the **Heckscher Playground (49)** *(Seventh Ave., W. 61st/W. 63rd Sts.)*. The biggest open space in the southern section of the park is the **Sheep Meadow (50)** *(starts at 66th St.)*, a designated quiet zone where sheep used to graze until as late as 1934. Nearby is **Strawberry Fields (51)** *(W. 72nd St at Central Park West)*, a former favorite spot of John Lennon, who lived in the Dakota apartments across from the park. If you're a Beatles fan it may be a must; if not, be warned: it's often full of guitar-twanging mourners paying tribute.

Mid-Park (72nd through 79th Sts.):

North and slightly east is **The Lake (52)**, with its

beautiful **Loeb Boathouse (53)** *(mid-park at 75th St.)* and charming **Bow Bridge (54)**. You can rent boats and even a gondola here. Near The Lake is the lovely **Bethesda Fountain and Terrace (55)** *(mid-park, by the 72nd St. Transverse Rd.)*, which is one of the social hives of the park, full of every type of character on earth on a hot summer's day. **The Ramble (56)** *(mid-park from 72nd through 79th Sts.)*, where pathways twist amongst brush and trees, is east of The Lake, and one of the best places for bird-watching. Just north of The Ramble are two architectural landmarks, the **Delacorte Theater (57)** *(mid-park at 80th St., see page 190)* and **Belvedere Castle (58)** *(mid-park at 79th St.)*—a Victorian stone block fantasy that rises majestically to the highest point in the park, offering superb views. It's also the location of the **Henry Luce Nature Observatory (58)** *(see page 189, hours: Tu–Su 10AM–5PM)*. As you move north over the 79th Street Transverse Road you come across a sweeping open expanse—**The Great Lawn (59)** *(mid-park, 79th/86th Sts.)*. A reservoir until the 1930s, it then became the place for New Yorkers to fool around—socializing, flirting, playing games, or just plain soaking up the sun. During the summer the Met and the Philharmonic stage free operas and concerts here, and The Lawn has played host to huge shows by the likes of Simon and Garfunkel and Garth Brooks. A reservoir still exists north of the 86th Street Transverse Road, now renamed **Jacqueline Kennedy Onassis Reservoir (60)** *(mid-park, 85th/96th Sts.)*. She was one of the thousands of people who used the popular jogging path around it, which is still in use.

North Section (97th through 110th Sts.):

North of the 97th Street Transverse Road at mid-park is the **North Meadow Recreation Center (61)**, a handsomely restored recreation facility set amidst the 23 acres of the North Meadow. The northernmost reaches of the park are some of the most beautiful and contrasting, with the wild beauty of the 11-acre **Harlem Meer (62)** *(NE corner of the park, 106th/109th Sts.)*, a lake where you can fish from mid-April through mid-October, and the formal landscaping of the **Conservatory Garden (63)** *(Fifth Ave. at E. 105th St., 212-360-2766; hours: 8AM–dusk)*.

Arts & Entertainment:

In Central Park it's hard to distinguish between kids' and adults' entertainment, so check out "Kids" on page 190 as well. For information on all activities, prices, and admission times, visit www.centralpark.org. If you're into fishing (strictly catch and release), the **Charles A. Dana Discovery Center (64)** *(Malcolm X Blvd. at 110th St., 212-860-1370)* will rent you equipment for fishing in nearby Harlem Meer. You can also meet up for bird-watching tours here, as well as take part in various family and children's workshops. Bird-watching and history tours also depart from the **Henry Luce Nature Observatory (58)**, which has microscopes, exhibits, and interactive displays for children, too. The **North Meadow Recreation Center (61)** *(mid-park at 97th St., 212-348-4867)* was converted from stables to a recreation center in the 1990s and offers soccer, softball, and 12 baseball fields for school and public use. Balls, bats, and other equipment can be rented inexpensively.

For culture lovers, there are the **summer outdoor music shows** *(see www.summerstage.org or www.centralparknyc. org for details)*, with everything from classical concerts by the New York Philharmonic to free rock concerts. Every summer the **Delacorte Theater (57)** *(mid-park at 80th St., www.publictheater.org)* presents its free annual Shakespeare in the Park Festival, featuring big name talent (e.g., Jimmy Smits, Patrick Stewart). There's also a host of other activities you can do, from chess to biking to blading. (Equipment for all three can be rented in the park.)

Kids:

The **Heckscher Playground (49)** *(Seventh Ave., 61st/63rd Sts.)* is the biggest playground in Central Park (three acres), filled with swings and other amusements, plus excellent bathrooms. The **Carousel (65)** *(mid-park at 65th St.)* offers rides on beautiful hand-painted wooden horses for three dollars; it's an attraction that's been going since 1871. The **Wollman Rink (46)** *(just north of the park entrance at Sixth Ave./59th St., www.wollmanskating rink.com, 212-439-6900)* is a year-round attraction

for children and adults alike. In the winter you can arrange for children's special skating classes with qualified teachers, and in the summer the rink is transformed into a delightful family center with a mini-carousel, rides, face

 painting, games, cotton candy, and all kinds of other attractions. The **Central Park Zoo (48)** *(830 Fifth Ave., 63rd/66th Sts., 212-439-6500, www.centralparkzoo.org),* of course, is the biggest children's attraction, and there are actually two of them—the **Tisch Children's Zoo (66)**, which is essentially a petting zoo with goats, sheep, and other domestic animals, and the main zoo itself, home to polar bears, sea lions, penguins, and much more, all painstakingly arranged in simulations of their natural habitats. If you can afford it, there are even overnight pajama parties for kids to learn about the animals. Avoid the lackluster food at the café.

PLACES TO EAT & DRINK
Where to Eat:

There are the classic hot dog and pretzel stands dotted around the park, or if you prefer a more upscale meal, try the **Central Park Boathouse Restaurant (67) ($$)** *(see Loeb Boathouse on page 188) (mid-park at 75th St., 212-517-2233; www.thecentralparkboathouse.com, hours: lunch year-round M–F 12PM–4PM; brunch year-round Sa–Su 9:30AM–4PM; dinner Apr–Nov M–F 5:30PM–9:30PM, Sa–Su 6PM–9:30PM).* It can be expensive and pretty limited, but the location can't be beat.

chapter 8

HARLEM & SPANISH HARLEM MORNINGSIDE HEIGHTS WASHINGTON HEIGHTS & INWOOD

Places to See:
1. Apollo Theater
2. Strivers' Row
3. Hamilton Heights Historic District
4. Abyssinian Baptist Church
5. Mount Morris Park
6. Trinity Cemetery
7. Graffiti Hall of Fame
8. Schomburg Center for Research in Black Culture
9. Studio Museum in Harlem
10. National Black Theater
11. Museo del Barrio
12. Museum of the City of New York
30. Cathedral Church of St. John the Divine
31. Columbia University
32. Low Memorial Library
33. Barnard College
34. Riverside Church
35. Grant's Tomb
45. George Washington Bridge
46. Fort Tryon Park
47. Cloisters Museum
48. Inwood Hill Park
49. Henry Hudson Bridge
50. Morris-Jumel Mansion

Places to Eat & Drink:
13. Amy Ruth's
14. Londel's Supper Club
15. Dinosaur Bar-B-Que
16. Uptown Juice Bar
17. Sylvia's
18. Red Rooster Harlem
19. Cotton Club
20. Lenox Lounge
21. Showman's Bar
22. Chocolat Restaurant Lounge
36. Kitchenette Uptown
37. Max Soha
38. Falafel on Broadway
39. Bistro Ten 18
40. Hungarian Pastry Shop
41. Le Monde
42. Heights Bar and Grill
51. New Leaf Café
52. Kismat Indian Restaurant

Sometimes I feel discriminated against,
but it does not make me angry.
It merely astonishes me.
How can anyone deny themselves
the pleasure of my company?

—Zora Neale Hurston

HARLEM & SPANISH HARLEM

HARLEM: **B** **C** *to 110th St.-Cathedral Parkway,*
116th St., 125th St., 135th St., 145th St.;
B **D** *to 155th St.;* **2** **3** *to Central Park North-*
110th St., 116th St., 125th St., 135th St.;
3 *to 145 St.;* **4** **5** **6** *to 125 St.*

SPANISH HARLEM: **6** *to 96th St., 103rd St.,*
110th St., 116th St., 125 St.; **4** **5** *to 125th St.*

● **SNAPSHOT** ●

Visitors to Manhattan often stop short north of Central
Park, or at the most take a trip to the Cloisters Museum
at Manhattan's far northern tip. That's a shame. The
numerous and varied neighborhoods of this area are
fascinating places to explore. Harlem *(110th St. to the
Harlem River, Morningside/Saint Nicholas Aves.)*, the
most famous, has been a center of African-American
life in New York since the early years of the 20th
century, and after a long period of turbulence in the
1960s and 1970s, is undergoing a major renaissance,
with its historic buildings being restored by new
owners (both black and white) and new
capital injected into its stores and businesses. Spanish Harlem *(E. 96th St.
to E. 120th Sts., approx., Fifth/
Third Aves.)*, or El Barrio
("The Neighborhood"), as it's
called by its largely Puerto

Rican population, has yet to attract the influx of capital that Harlem has, but is still well worth visiting for its street life and delicious, inexpensive food.

PLACES TO SEE
Landmarks:

One of the most famous landmarks is the **Apollo Theater (1)** *(253 W. 125th St., Adam Clayton Powell Jr. Blvd./Frederick Douglass Blvd., 212-531-5300, www.apollotheater.org)*. It was here that Michael Jackson, Ella Fitzgerald, and a host of other R&B and soul stars got their start. Amateur Night at the Apollo is a funny and enjoyable musical contest to watch, but is brutal for contestants the audience doesn't like. The tree stump that performers touch for good luck before singing came from the "Tree of Hope" that once grew outside Harlem's Lafayette Theatre. Harlem has some of the best 19th-century residential architecture in the country, now in a flurry of restoration in many places. Check out **Strivers' Row (2)** *(W. 138th to W. 139th Sts., Powell/Douglass Blvds.)*, a block of beautiful Renaissance-style brick row houses, designed in part by McKim, Mead & White in 1890. As the area became increasingly African-American, the black middle classes moved into the block and the term "Strivers' Row" gained popular usage. The other major area for handsome row houses is in the **Hamilton Heights Historic District (3)** *(W. 140th/W. 145th Sts., Amsterdam/Edgecomb Aves.)*. In particular, note the lovely houses on Convent Avenue, near W. 148th Street, with their curving stoops and bay windows. The **Abyssinian Baptist Church (4)** *(132 Odell Clark Pl., formerly West 138th St., Adam Clayton Powell, Jr./Malcolm X Blvds., also known as 7th and Lenox Aves., 212-862-7474, www.abyssinian.org)* is the most well-known of Harlem's numerous churches and offers wonderful services with gospel singing. If you're interested in gospel tours of Harlem, many companies offer them, generally with brunch or drinks included. (Note that large groups are required to register with this and other churches in advance, especially on Sundays.) Harlem has several lovely parks and open spaces, and **Mount Morris Park (5)** *(W. 120th/W. 124th Sts., Madison Ave./ Mount Morris Park West, www.mmpcia.org)*, also known as Marcus Garvey Park, is the most historic. Only a few years ago many of the houses surrounding it were simply shells, or grimly hanging on as rooming houses, but the establishment of a Historic District and the recent frenzy of restoration, has restored these buildings to their original splendor. **Trinity Cemetery (6)** *(W. 153rd/W. 155th Sts., Riverside Dr./ Amsterdam Ave.)* has some of the oldest graves in the city (including those of notable New Yorkers John James Audubon and John Jacob Astor), with great views over the Hudson River. In Spanish Harlem, check out the **Graffiti Hall of Fame (7)** *(W. 106th St., Madison/Park Aves.)*, where the long walls are covered in brilliantly colored images by masters, old-school and otherwise.

Arts & Entertainment:

As befits a neighborhood so rich in cultural history—with figures such as writers Zora Neale Hurston and Langston Hughes, and musicians Fats Waller, Duke Ellington, and Louis Armstrong; all lived or worked there in the 1920s and 1930s—Harlem has a large number of first-class cultural institutions. Its musical heritage is kept alive in its clubs and bars *(see page 200)*, but for a general cultural record of black America the **Schomburg Center for Research in Black Culture (8)** *(515 Malcolm X Blvd. at W. 135th St., 917-275-6975, www.nypl.org/locations/schomburg; hours: M 10AM–6PM, Tu–Th 10AM–8PM, Sa 10AM–6PM)* can't be beat. The center offers a permanent collection of documents, books, films, and more, and excellent exhibitions—a genuinely moving and informative experience. The **Studio Museum in Harlem (9)** *(144 W. 125th St., Malcolm X/Adam Clayton Powell Jr. Blvds., 212-864-4500, www.studiomuseum.org, cash only; hours: Th–F 12PM–9PM, Sa 10AM–6PM, Su 12PM–6PM)* was founded in 1968 to exhibit work by black artists, both American and foreign. It offers lecture series, artists in residence, and varied exhibitions by painters, sculptors, and more. The gift shop is top notch. The **National Black Theater (10)** *(2031 Fifth Ave., W. 125th/W. 126th Sts., 212-722-3800, www.nationalblacktheatre.org)* is an enormous 64,000 square-foot building that's broken up inside into a number of much smaller, more intimate performing areas, decorated with African art and decor. Plays and other forms of performances here emphasize black culture and history. Spanish Harlem has its own equivalent to the Studio Museum in Harlem, the **Museo del Barrio (11)**

(1230 Fifth Ave., E. 104th/E. 105th Sts., 212-831-7272, www.elmuseo.org; hours: Tu–Sa 11AM–6PM). It has a large and varied collection of works by Latino artists, both living abroad and resident in the U.S., as well as excellent temporary exhibits. The **Museum of the City of New York (12)** *(1220 Fifth Ave., E. 103rd/E. 104th Sts., 212-534-1672, www.mcny.org; hours: daily 10AM–6PM)* houses a delightful collection of artifacts that reveal the history of the city from colonial times to the present, including photographs, paintings, and documents. There's also a touching collection of more personal effects such as children's toys, diaries, and other ephemera.

PLACES TO EAT & DRINK
Where to Eat:

Don't come to Harlem expecting to eat light: soul food is the name of the game here, and it's the best in the city. At **Amy Ruth's (13) ($)** *(113 W. 116th St., Lenox/Seventh Aves., 212-280-8779, www.amyruthsharlem.com; hours: M 11:30AM–11PM, Tu–Th 8:30AM–11PM, F 8:30AM–5:30AM, Sa 7:30AM–5:30AM, Su 7:30AM–11PM)* portions are big, prices are fair, and there's a waffle dish named after Rev. Al Sharpton. **Londel's Supper Club (14) ($$)** *(2620 Frederick Douglass Blvd., W. 139th/W. 140th Sts., 212-234-6114, www.londelsrestaurant.com; hours: Tu–Sa 5PM–11PM, Su 11AM–5PM)* does a sterling Sunday brunch and has some of the best soul food in town. If you're in the mood for barbeque, head to **Dinosaur Bar-B-Que (15) ($)** *(700 W. 125th St. at 12th Ave., 212-694-1777, www.dinosaurbarbque.com; hours: M–Th 11:30AM–11PM, F–Sa 11:30AM–12AM, Su*

12PM–10PM) for your fill of fried green tomatoes, creole spiced deviled eggs, and lots of other tasty, finger-lickin' grub. Get your okra, collards, and mac'n'cheese at the vegetarian Caribbean spot **Uptown Juice Bar (16) ($)** *(14 E. 125th St., Madison/5th Aves., 212-987-2660; hours: daily 8AM–10PM).* They make a mean honey-barbequed tofu—who said you can't have veggie BBQ with some soul? **Sylvia's (17) ($)** *(328 Lenox Ave., 126th/127th Sts., 212-996-0660, www.sylviasrestaurant.com; hours: M–Sa 8AM–10:30PM, Su 11AM–8PM)* opened in 1962 with a seating capacity of 35. It now seats up to 450 and is a world-famous historic restaurant serving up soul food classics. Neighborhood resident—and celebrated chef—Marcus Samuelsson's **Red Rooster Harlem (18) ($$)** *(310 Lenox Ave., 125th/126th Sts., 212-792-9001; www.redroosterharlem.com; hours: brunch Sa–Su 10AM–3PM, lunch M–F 11:30AM–3PM, dinner M–Th 5:30PM–10:30PM, F 5:30PM–11:30PM, Sa 5PM–11:30PM, Su 5PM–10PM)* is always a fun scene, particularly the gospel Sunday brunch. The restaurant pays homage to traditional American food.

Bars & Nightlife:

Harlem is hopping with nightlife, and historic jazz venues. Call ahead or visit the clubs' websites for specific showtimes. The tiny **Cotton Club (19)** *(656 W. 125th St. at Riverside Dr., 212-663-7980, www.cotton club-newyork.com, hours: M, Th–F dinner starts 8PM; Sa brunch seatings at 12PM and 2:30PM, dinner starts 9PM; Su brunch seatings at 12PM and 2:30PM)* has a great band and offers dining and cocktails as well as brunch specials.

There's swing dancing every Monday night. (This isn't the 1923 Cotton Club, but a newer venture established in 1978.) The **Lenox Lounge (20)** *(333 Lenox Ave., W. 127th St., 212-427-0253, www.lenoxlounge.com)*, moved two blocks from its original location, and its Deco decor and live jazz send you on a serious time trip. **Showman's Bar (21)** *(375 W. 125th St., St. Nicholas/Morningside Aves., 212-864-8941)*, established in 1942, is one of Harlem's genuine jazz treasures; drinks are inexpensive and it's all about the music here. With its cozy, inviting interior and imaginative cocktail list, **Chocolat Restaurant Lounge (22)** *(2217-23 Frederick Douglass Blvd., at 120th St., 212-222-4545, www.chocolatharlem.com; hours: M–Th 11AM–11PM, F 11AM–3AM, Sa 10AM–3AM, Su 11AM–10PM)* is the perfect place for an intimate dinner for two, or a quiet drink with friends.

WHERE TO SHOP

Along with the revival of many classic neighborhood buildings comes the arrival of some of the more soulless commercial glitz of downtown, such as the vast Harlem USA Complex (23) *(300 W. 125th St., Adam Clayton Powell Jr./Frederick Douglass Blvds.)*, though if you want the latest sneakers or street wear it comes in handy. For more personal stores check out the open-air Malcolm Shabazz Harlem Market (24) *(52 W. 116th St. at Malcolm X Blvd., 212-987-8131; hours: daily 10AM–8PM)*, which sells wonderful African fabrics, clothes, and crafts. For more sports equipment and gear, check out House of Hoops (25) *(268 W. 125th St., at Frederick Douglass Blvd., 212-316-1667, www.houseofhoops.com; hours: M–F 9AM–8PM,*

Sa–Su 10AM–7PM), which carries the top brands for both amateurs and pros. If your style tends toward the dapper, check out Harlem Haberdashery (26) (*245 Lenox Ave., 122nd/123rd Sts., 646-707-0070, www.harlem haberdashery.com; hours: daily 11:30AM–8:30PM*). A new uptown boutique, Harlem Haberdashery draws inspiration from the rich cultural history and distinctive style of the Harlem Renaissance, while adding a future-forward edge to their exclusive designs. The result is a classic silhouette set off by a definitive expression of today's fashion. In Spanish Harlem, the main shopping strip is along East 116th Street (27). There are plenty of small food vendors and stores known as botanicas, that sell candles and religious charms and icons. They're well worth visiting because botanicas are disappearing at a fast rate in the city as real estate developments roll over them.

WHERE TO STAY

Harlem has a number of bed-and-breakfast inns, which are an intimate and easy way to get a feel for the neighborhood. The Sugar Hill Harlem Inn (28) ($$-$$$) (*460 W. 141st St., Amsterdam/Convent Aves., 212-234-5432, www.sugarhillharleminn.com*) features rooms that are named after great artists associated with the area, such as "Ella's Room" and "Satchmo's Room." The 1906 Victorian town house has been beautifully restored to preserve the historical details of the building. The Harlem Flophouse (29) ($) (*242 W. 123rd St., 347-632-1960, www.harlemflophouse.com*) is even more reasonably priced in another handsomely restored old building. There's a communal dining room and garden.

MORNINGSIDE HEIGHTS

B **C** *to Cathedral Parkway-110th St., 116th St.,*
125th St.; **1** *to Cathedral Parkway-110th St.,*
116th St.-Columbia University, 125th St.

● **SNAPSHOT** ●

Morningside Heights, nicknamed the Academic Acropolis thanks to the number of educational institutions in the area, including Columbia University and Barnard College, is the closest thing you'll find to a "college town" in New York City. This makes it an ideal place to stroll while checking out the wonderful campus buildings and the inexpensive bars, cafés, and restaurants that cluster around them. The main shopping and eating drag is Broadway from 110th to 116th streets, though there are many places tucked away in the side streets.

PLACES TO SEE
Landmarks:

A great landmark here—one of New York's finest—is the truly astonishing **Cathedral Church of St. John the Divine (30)** *(1047 Amsterdam Ave. at 112th St., 212-316-7540, www.stjohndivine.org)*. St. John's size has to be seen to be believed; it's bigger than Notre Dame and Chartres cathedrals in France combined, and the Statue of Liberty would fit beneath her dome. Her famous Rose Window is the largest stained-glass window in the country. St. John's was begun in 1892 and is still far from finished, as the empty niches on the exterior make clear.

Teams of sculptors are still working on her today, and as a result the church represents a number of architectural styles. Tours of the grounds and interior are available. If you're here in October, don't miss the annual Blessing of the Animals as part of the Feast of St. Francis, when animals from horses and snakes to gerbils and rats parade up the aisle with their owners. The major academic institution here is **Columbia University (31)** *(main entrance: Broadway at W. 116th St., 212-854-1754, www.colum bia.edu)*, designed by Charles McKim of the famous architectural firm McKim, Mead & White in grand Beaux Arts style. The centerpiece is the **Low Memorial Library (32)**, a classical porticoed temple around which the other campus buildings are clustered. The campus is open to the public, though you need to be part of the regular student-led tours to visit the interior elements. Visitors should head to the Visitors Center in the Low Library for information. Across the street is **Barnard College (33)** *(main entrance: Broadway bet. W. 116/W. 120 Sts., www.barnard.edu)*, a private women's liberal arts college affiliated with Columbia. **Riverside Church (34)** *(490 Riverside Dr. at W. 120th St., 212-870-6700, www.theriversidechurchny.org; hours: daily 7AM–10PM)*, a Rockefeller-funded project that rises 21 stories, has a not-to-be-missed observation deck in its bell tower. **Grant's Tomb (35)** *(Riverside Dr. at W. 122nd St., www. nps.gov/gegr; hours: W–M 10AM–5PM)*, formerly known as the General Grant National Memorial, was the city's number one tourist attraction in the early years of the 20th century. Its attraction has waned, but this domed classical monument is still worth a visit.

PLACES TO EAT & DRINK
Where to Eat:

Tom's Restaurant (61) *(2880 Broadway, W. 112 St., 212-864-6137, www.tomsrestaurant.net; hours: Su–W 6AM–1:30AM, 24HRS Th–Sa)* is famous for being the stand-in for the fictional Monk's Café in the television sitcom *Seinfeld* and is a popular student-hangout because of its cheap diner food, delicious shakes, and homey atmosphere. **Kitchenette Uptown (36) ($)** *(1272 Amsterdam Ave., W. 122nd/W. 123rd Sts., 212-531-7600, www.kitchenetterestaurant.com; hours: M–F 8AM–11PM, Sa–Su 9AM–11PM)* is a tiny spot and a favorite with college students and others on a tight budget who want a meal with a homemade feel but a chef's touch. Next door there's **Max Soha (37) ($$)** *(1274 Amsterdam Ave. at W. 123rd St., 212-531-2221, www.maxsoha.com, cash only; hours: daily 12PM–12AM)*, serving can't-go-wrong Italian food at great prices, though its popularity means the lines can be long. Awnings sporting dark colors and bright (or, over time, dingy) white lettering are a nondescript signature style of NYC—but some welcome eaters to great delights. Stop into the not-fancy-but-so-very-good **Falafel on Broadway (38) ($)** *(3151 Broadway at Tiemann Pl., 212-222-2300; hours: daily 11AM–12AM)* for the namesake treat, gyros, and kebabs aplenty. On 110th Street there's the excellent **Bistro Ten 18 (39) ($$)** *(1018 Amsterdam Ave. at W. 110th St., 212-662-7600, www. bistroten18.com: M–F 4PM–11PM, Sa 11AM–3PM and 5PM–11PM, Su 11AM–3PM and 5PM–10PM)* for simple well-produced American fare with a great view of the

Cathedral Church of St. John the Divine (30). The **Hungarian Pastry Shop (40) ($)** *(1030 Amsterdam Ave., W. 110th/W. 111th Sts., 212-866-4230; hours: M–F 8AM–11:30PM, Sa 8:30AM–11:30PM, Su 8:30AM–10:30PM)* is an Eastern European classic in the heart of college town. You can't beat its *sacher tortes* and *linzer tarts*, washed down with strong Viennese coffee.

Bars & Nightlife:

An amble down Broadway between about W. 110th and W. 116th streets reveals a large number of bars and cafés, all frequented by Columbia students and faculty. **Le Monde (41)** *(2885 Broadway, W. 112th/W. 113th Sts., 212-531-3939, www.lemondenyc.com; hours: M–Th 11AM–4PM, F 11AM–12PM, Sa 9:30AM–12PM, Su 9:30AM–12AM)* is a certified-green brasserie with good beer and atmosphere. The **Heights Bar and Grill (42)** *(2867 Broadway, W. 111th/W. 112th Sts., 212-866-7035, www.theheights nyc.com; hours: bar open daily until 3AM)* has a (teensy) rooftop bar and offers cheap Mexican food washed down with margaritas.

WHERE TO SHOP

Mondel Chocolates (43) *(2913 Broadway at W. 114th St., 212-864-2111, www.mondelchocolates.com; hours: M–Sa 11AM–7PM)* has been going since 1943, and its old-fashioned vibe is the secret to its success. The Bank Street Bookstore (44) *(610 W. 112th St. at Broadway, 212-678-1654, www.bankstreetbooks.com; hours: M–F 9AM–8PM, Sa–Su 10AM–8PM)* is an excellent children's bookstore with a highly knowledgeable staff.

WASHINGTON HEIGHTS & INWOOD

WASHINGTON HEIGHTS: **C** *to 155th St., 163rd St.-Amsterdam Ave., 168th St.-Washington Heights;* **A** *to 168th St.-Washington Heights, 175th St., 181st St., 190th St., Dyckman St.;* **1** *to 157th St., 168th St., 181st St., 191st St., Dyckman St.*

INWOOD: **A** *to Inwood-207th St.;* **1** *to 207th St., 215th St.*

● SNAPSHOT ●

Most New Yorkers live their entire lives never knowing what lies at Manhattan's northern tip. The answer is some of the best parks in the city, one of its best museums, great street life, and views of the Hudson River and the New Jersey Palisades that can't be beat. It's definitely worth the trip. Washington Heights *(W. 155th/Dyckman, a.k.a. 200th, St., between the Hudson and Harlem Rivers)* and Inwood *(north of Dyckman St. between the Hudson and Harlem Rivers)* both used to be the sites of large estates and remained among the last parts of New York to be urbanized until the subway systems reached them in the 1930s. Washington Heights is home to one of the largest Dominican populations in the city. But its parks and handsome apartment buildings have seen many

new residents in recent years, especially young artists, forced northward by ever-escalating real estate prices. At its northern end is Fort Tryon Park, laid out by Frederick Law Olmsted (son of the Olmsted of Central Park fame) and home to the stunning Cloisters Museum, where the Metropolitan Museum maintains its medieval collection. Inwood has a relatively small residential population and a beautiful park, Inwood Hill Park, where some of the last primeval forest in Manhattan can be found.

PLACES TO SEE
Landmarks:

The **George Washington Bridge (45)** *(spanning the Hudson River at 179th St.),* one of New York's most amazing pieces of engineering (and lit up beautifully at night), can best be viewed from Fort Washington Avenue, which runs parallel to the waterfront. The virgin peaks on the far side, known as the Palisades, which are at their best in the fall, were bought up by the Rockefeller family to prevent development, perhaps the greatest of their many philanthropic acts. Washington Avenue eventually leads to **Fort Tryon Park (46)** *(W. 190th St. to Riverside Dr.),* a park that combines careful landscaping with the wild and rocky natural topography of the site. In the summer it's a favorite spot for weddings, and the views of both the city to the east and the Palisades across the river are breathtaking. The park is home to the **Cloisters Museum (47)** *(see page 209),* a branch of The

Metropolitan Museum of Art. **Inwood Hill Park (48)** *(north and west of Dyckman St. to the tip of Manhattan)* is the supposed site of original Dutch governor Peter Minuit's "purchase" of Manhattan from the Native American Lenapes in 1626, or so a plaque here will inform you. The park is densely filled in places with the last vestiges of the forest that once covered Manhattan from tip to tip. At the very northern end is the **Henry Hudson Bridge (49)**, and painted on the rocks nearby is the vast blue "C," for Columbia University, whose students play soccer and football at nearby Baker Field.

Arts & Entertainment:
The **Cloisters Museum (47)** *(Fort Washington Ave. at Margaret Corbin Plaza, 212-923-3700, www.met museum.org; hours: March–Oct daily 10AM–5:15PM; Nov–Feb daily 10AM–4:45PM)* is a miracle of money and vision. In the 1930s the Rockefeller family, which owned the land that's now Fort Tryon Park, purchased, shipped back home, and reassembled elements of five medieval cloisters from Europe. The Met now houses its medieval art collection here, but the real attraction is this exquisite architectural sanctuary, perhaps the most peaceful spot in all of New York City. Another lovely museum in this neighborhood is the **Morris-Jumel Mansion (50)** *(65 Jumel Terrace, W. 160th/W. 162nd Sts., 212-923-8008, www.morrisjumel.org; hours: W–Su 10AM–4PM, M–Tu by appointment only),* the oldest house in Manhattan and home to George Washington during parts of the Revolutionary War. It offers excellent tours of the house and grounds, as well as a number of children's programs.

PLACES TO EAT & DRINK
Where to Eat:

If you're visiting The Cloisters, the **New Leaf Café (51)** *(1 Margaret Corbin Dr. near Park Dr., 212-568-5323, www.newleafrestaurant.com; hours: lunch M–F*  *12PM–3:30PM, dinner Tu–Th, Su 6PM–9PM, F–Sa 6PM–10PM, brunch Sa–Su 11AM–3:30PM)* is a great place to stop for a bite. The restaurant's views—there's a pleasant open-air terrace to enjoy in good weather—bring people back. Profits go toward Fort Tryon Park. Need curry in a hurry? In the Washington Heights area, you can pop into the popular **Kismat Indian Restaurant (52) ($)** *(603 Fort Washington Ave., at 187th St., 212-795-8633; hours: daily 11:30AM–11PM)*, a neighborhood institution. The menu is a mix of American, Southwest, and Cajun at **107 West (53) ($-$$)** *(811 W. 187th St., 212-864-1555, www.107west.com; call for hours)*. The fried chicken has fans.

Bars & Nightlife:

Washington Heights has always had a buzzing street life at night, but with gentrification has come a hip bar scene. The tiny **Locksmith Wine & Burger Bar (54)** *(4463 Broadway bet. Fairview Ave./192nd St., 212-304-9463; hours: M–W 3PM–2AM, Th–F 3PM–4AM, Sa–Su 12PM–4AM)* offers an excellent drink selection, tasty food, and a calm break from this hectic stretch of Broadway. The **Monkey Room Bar (55)** *(589 Fort*

Washington Ave. at W. 187th St., 212-543-9888; hours: daily 3PM–4AM) is a hip, eclectic spot that serves as a morning coffee shop as well as a DJ-heavy nightclub.

WHERE TO SHOP

For those with literary or artistic interests, Word Up Books (56) *(2113 Amsterdam Ave. at 165th St., 347-688-4456, www.wordupbooks.com; hours: Tu–F 3PM–9PM, Sa 11AM–8PM, Su 12PM–6PM)* is a multilingual, general-interest community bookshop and arts space, whose mission is to support and fortify the creative spirit in this diverse community. The Met has one of the best gift shops of all museums, and its branch at the Cloisters, Cloisters Gift Shop (57) *(see Cloisters Museum on page 209)* has plenty of fun medieval kitsch to take home as a memento. Or pick up a tasty memento at Carrot Top Pastries (58) *(3931 Broadway, 164th/165th Sts., 212-927-4800, www.carrottoppastries.com; M–Sa 6AM–9PM, Su 7AM–6PM)*, which arguably bakes up the best carrot cake in town, as well as other delectables. Fashion, music, and art merge to create the high-end street wear available at Probus (59) *(714 W. 181st St., Bennett Ave./Broadway, 212-923-9153, www.probusnyc.com; hours: M–Sa 10AM–8PM, Su 12:30PM–7:30PM)*. Designer foot-wear, jeans, sunglasses, and more will have you looking smooth and stylish. If you're looking for authentic Latin tunes, *baile* (dance) your way over to Quisqueya (60) *(52 Sherman Ave., Arden/Thayer Sts., 212-942-1020; hours: M–Sa 10AM–8PM, Su 12PM–8PM)*. From salsa to meringue, and bachata to bolero, they stock over 25,000 CDs and records, including rare out-of-print albums. *Viva musica!*

INDEX

NOTES

NOTES

NOTES

NOTES

NOTES

NOTES

PETER PAUPER PRESS
Fine Books and Gifts Since 1928

Our Company

In 1928, at the age of twenty-two, Peter Beilenson began printing books on a small press in the basement of his parents' home in Larchmont, New York. Peter—and later, his wife, Edna—sought to create fine books that sold at "prices even a pauper could afford."

Today, still family owned and operated, Peter Pauper Press continues to honor our founders' legacy—and our customers' expectations—of beauty, quality, and value.

While in New York, don't forget to visit the **New York Transit Museum** *(corner of Boerum Place and Schermerhorn Street, Subway: A, C, G to Hoyt-Schermerhorn, 1-718-694-1600, www.mta.info/mta/museum, hours: Tu-F 10AM-4PM, Sa-Su noon-5PM).* Housed in a historic 1936 IND subway station (which is, of course, easily accessible by subway), this is the largest museum in the United States devoted to urban public transportation history. Exhibits explore the social and practical impact of public transportation on the development of greater New York; among the highlights is an engrossing walk-through display carting the construction of the city's century-old subway system, when fearless 'sandhogs' were engaged in dangerous tunneling. A line-up of turnstyles shows their evolution from the 1894 'ticket chopper' to the current Automatic Fare Card model. But the best part is down another level to a real platform where you can board an exceptional collection of vintage subway and El ('Elevated') cars, some complete with vintage ads. Admission is $7 for adults, $5 for children 2-17, $5 for seniors (62+). Free Wednesdays. Free for Museum members. If you're in Grand Central Terminal, be sure to visit the New York Transit Museum Gallery Annex & Store *(1-212-878-0106),* located in the main concourse.